PRAISE FOR JOLT!

"Phil Cooke can help you make disruption and change the source of your success—not the end of it. *Jolt!* offers practical tips on how to manage circumstances, emotions, and unforeseen changes to your advantage. Read it and embrace your new reality."

—TIM SANDERS, FORMER CHIEF SOLUTIONS OFFICER AT
YAHOO! AND AUTHOR OF *LOVE IS THE KILLER APP*

"*Jolt!* may be the best book yet from one of the most innovative communicators of our generation. In this sure-to-be best seller, Phil Cooke deals with the issue of change in a way that allows us to embrace it rather than fear it, to benefit from it rather than to be hurt by it, and to harness it as a means of achieving a real and positive change in every area of our life. This book is for everyone."

—JOEL OSTEEN, SENIOR PASTOR, LAKEWOOD CHURCH, HOUSTON, TX

"*Jolt!* will motivate you to adapt and change to our ever evolving world . . . Phil Cooke's clear and frank writing style speaks directly to today's readers, applicable for both personal and business sides of us all."

—MARK ZORADI, FORMER PRESIDENT OF
WALT DISNEY MOTION PICTURE GROUP

"The world has changed and nothing will ever be the same again. Most people have reacted by hunkering down and settling into survival mode. In *Jolt!* Phil Cooke brilliantly shows us that we were created for something far greater. We don't have to have life dictated to us. We can rise above the chaos and stay ahead of the curve."

—STEVEN FURTICK, LEAD PASTOR, ELEVATION
CHURCH; AUTHOR OF *SUN STAND STILL*

"In today's fast-paced world, nothing stays static for long. *Jolt!* provides smart ideas on how to embrace change in a tangible and powerful way."

—DAN LIN, PRODUCER OF *SHERLOCK HOLMES* 1 & 2, AND
EXECUTIVE PRODUCER OF *TERMINATOR SALVATION*

"Phil Cooke will jolt your world. He does mine. This is why when our ministry wants to fast forward, we talk to Phil. *Jolt!* puts in your head a lifetime of Phil's best ideas. It will rock your world and change the way you think."

—PASTOR JACK GRAHAM, PRESTONWOOD CHURCH AND
FOUNDER OF POWERPOINT MINISTRIES

"Phil Cooke has to be one of the greatest voices in our world today to address the topics he brings out in his book *Jolt! Get the Jump on a World That's Constantly Changing*. His experience in industry and in religion combine to give him a powerful perspective on culture. I believe that our ability to communicate with our constantly changing world will hinge on understanding and acting on the truths Phil writes in this book. Phil is helping me and our organization to get to jumping!"

—DINO RIZZO, LEAD PASTOR, HEALING PLACE CHURCH, DINORIZZO.COM

"When I created the nationwide Get Motivated Seminars, one of my driving passions was to help professionals understand today's rapidly changing business world. *Jolt!* is a road map for understanding those changes. If you're serious about success, this is the book I recommend."

—PETER LOWE, FOUNDER OF THE GET MOTIVATED SEMINARS

"Change is no longer an option but a fact of life. *Jolt!* will help you to decide, implement, and process the changes you need to make that will take you to the next level. Phil Cooke is one of the most creative, innovative, provocative and out of the box thinkers and leaders I know. This book is an essential tool for you and your organization."

—CHRISTINE CAINE, WRITER, SPEAKER, AND FOUNDER OF THE A21 CAMPAIGN

"Today's ever-changing and fast paced world can be overwhelming. *Jolt!* offers unique and inspiring solutions to problems that arise in the busy and chaotic times we live in. It will equip you with the tools to move forward in life with new passion and determination."

—JOYCE MEYER, BIBLE TEACHER AND BEST-SELLING AUTHOR

"In the 21st century we are all facing the very real and sometimes confronting elements of change. An ever-changing society has effects on the way we live life, do business and navigate our faith. Phil Cooke is a scholar of culture, a lover of people and passionate about seeing everyone reach their God-given potential and I believe that his insights on change will help you to fulfill yours."

—BRIAN HOUSTON, SENIOR PASTOR, HILLSONG CHURCH

"No one can argue that our world is changing—fast. But many of us simply don't know how to keep pace with the change, much less what we can do to change ourselves. In *Jolt!* Phil Cooke shows not only how we can live with constant change, but harness it."

—PASTOR GREG SURRATT, SEACOAST CHURCH:

"If life is a speeding car, Phil Cooke is the guy in the passenger seat, yelling out all the monuments as you blow by them. "Jolt" is a bracing tour of an ever-changing landscape. But the book is also filled with countless "pull over to the side of the road, old-fashioned picnic basket" kind of moments, as well . . . where wisdom is for lunch and insight for dessert. You may not agree with everything Phil has to say, but you'll be very glad you brought him along for the ride."

—TODD KOMARNICKI, PRODUCER OF THE MOVIE "ELF"

"Once again, Phil Cooke brings clarity and insight as he illustrates how we can navigate the unsettling seas of today's technological onslaught. *Jolt!* is an intelligent road map."

—TONY THOMOPOULOS, FORMER PRESIDENT OF ABC BROADCAST
GROUP AND FORMER CHAIRMAN OF UNITED ARTIST PICTURES

"You can reach your goals and achieve your dreams with Phil Cooke's *Jolt!* Get ready to take control of your destiny."

—HOWARD KAZANJIAN, PRODUCER OF *RAIDERS OF THE LOST
ARK* AND *STAR WARS EPISODE VI: THE RETURN OF THE JEDI*

"The world that we live in has increased its pace at a considerable rate. Phil Cooke gives us the "jolt" we need to prepare ourselves for the future. Old habits are just that—old. You must change and continue to change, or you will be left behind. Now is the time to prepare. Are you ready? Is your team ready? *Jolt!* will stimulate your skills, influence your legacy, and help you complete a blockbuster life!"

—SAMUEL SMITH, CHIEF EXECUTIVE OFFICER, MERCY SHIPS

"Phil Cooke lives and breathes relevance; he is like the lead explorer who goes ahead of the pack sees what is ahead and then he calls out to the rest to follow. In this book he does just that: he speaks to everyone who seeks to be relevant to a constantly changing culture and says this is the road to effectiveness in communicating the truth. Read it, you will be challenged and provoked to explore new possibilities"

—MICHAEL YOUSSEF PhD, HOST OF THE
GLOBAL MEDIA PROGRAM LEADING THE WAY.

"The only way to hit a moving target (and Phil Cooke shows just how fast-moving this culture is) is to get ahead of it. If you're tired of playing the game of either catch-up or put-down, *Jolt!* is for you. It's the best book out there on how to move from carpe diem to carpe mañana."

—LEONARD SWEET, BEST-SELLING AUTHOR AND PROFESSOR
(DREW UNIVERSITY, GEORGE FOX UNIVERSITY)

"Phil Cooke is on the cutting edge, bringing to the body of Christ new ideas and strategies for proclaiming the gospel. He has successfully guided hundreds of churches and ministries into this brave new world of marketing and technology. The message of the gospel never changes, but the way it's proclaimed should!"
—PAUL CROUCH JR., CHIEF OF STAFF, TRINITY BROADCASTING NETWORK

"*Jolt!* is like a slap in the face that causes you to pause and reflect on how we have become entrapped by "disruptive" technologies. It lays out a coherent plan to aid you in overcoming these distractions and to achieve success in your personal life as well as your career. This book is a road map to regain your freedom: physically, emotionally, and spiritually."
—ARTHUR ANDERSON, PRODUCER, *MISSION IMPOSSIBLE III*

"Phil Cooke is one of today's most sensitive, sensible, and savvy men I know in the arena of media communications and production. His grasp of how to capture the attention of the public or a specific audience as well as to assist ready observers, readers, or listeners with resources will make them glad they tuned in to his message."
—JACK W. HAYFORD, CHANCELLOR AND FOUNDER, THE KING'S UNIVERSITY, LOS ANGELES, CALIFORNIA

"It will wake you up . . . with a *Jolt!* Phil surveys the disrupted landscape and then finds a number of important minor and major ways to cope with life in the age of "tap and watch and react." Addressing our challenges with personal importance, growth, and power, Phil shows how many problems can be made worse through our best efforts. Without the biblical notions of trust, forgiveness, and good thinking, we will miss the blessings of progress in communications and just bog down in a narcissistic social networking."
— ANDREW J. PETERSON, PRESIDENT, REFORMED THEOLOGICAL SEMINARY, VIRTUAL CAMPUS, CHARLOTTE, NC

"Don't miss Jolt. It's jam-packed with practical wisdom for today's fast-changing world. Phil Cooke is a modern-day Solomon."
— MICHAEL LEE STALLARD, PRESIDENT, E PLURIBUS PARTNERS; AUTHOR, *FIRED UP OR BURNED OUT*

JOLT!

JOLT!

GET THE JUMP
ON A WORLD THAT'S
CONSTANTLY CHANGING

by Phil Cooke

THOMAS NELSON
Since 1798

NASHVILLE   DALLAS   MEXICO CITY   RIO DE JANEIRO

Jolt!

Published in Nashville, Tennessee, by Thomas Nelson. Thomas Nelson is a trademark of Thomas Nelson, Inc.

The author is represented by and this book is published in association with the literary agency of WordServe Literary Group, Ltd., www.wordserveliterary.com.

Thomas Nelson, Inc., titles may be purchased in bulk for educational, business, fund-raising, or sales promotional use. For information, please e-mail SpecialMarkets@ThomasNelson.com.

Page design by Mandi Cofer

ISBN 978-1-59554-773-6 (IE)

Library of Congress Cataloging-in-Publication Data

Cooke, Phil.
   Jolt! : get the jump on a world that's constantly changing / by Phil Cooke.
      p. cm.
   ISBN 978-1-59555-324-9
   1. Change (Psychology) I. Title.
BF637.C4C67 2010
158.1—dc22

2010034330

Printed in the United States of America
11 12 13 14 15 QGF 6 5 4 3 2 1

To Kathleen

CONTENTS

Contents

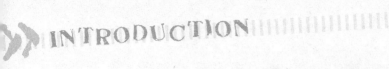

INTRODUCTION

LIVING IN A DISRUPTED WORLD

Jolt: To disturb. To shock. To interfere with abruptly. To shake things up.

I don't have to convince you the world is changing. Globalization has changed business, the media have changed our perceptions, culture has changed our values, and technology has changed everything. We live in the instant world of mobile phones, text messaging, and social networking. In the digital universe, word travels fast and change is overwhelming, often happening without warning.

For better or worse, *disruption* is the word that best describes twenty-first-century living.

But the question is, as the world around us changes, have *we* changed? How have we adapted to the turmoil that surrounds our lives? Perhaps more important, have our personal lives kept pace with radically escalating technology?

You're about to begin a journey that will have enormous impact on your life. The principles of this book will work for those with a passion to change their company, their community, or their lives. From corporate CEOs to rising visionaries to housewives, this book could be the answer you've been looking for. In a world where the very foundations you've believed in all your life are crumbling, how do you move forward toward your purpose?

Sure, everyone tells us we *need* to change, but how do we actually do it? Especially in a world where it seems as if the rules are just being made up? And it's not getting any easier.

> » **DISRUPTION IS NOT JUST THEORETICAL;**
> **IT'S PERSONAL.**

According to John Freeman, author of *The Tyranny of E-mail*:

- 65 percent of North Americans spend more time with their computer than their spouse.
- E-mail is addictive in the same way slot machines have been shown to be addictive.
- In 2009, it's been estimated, the average corporate worker spent more than 40 percent of his or her day sending or receiving some 200 e-mail messages.
- Information overload is a $650 billion drag on our economy each year.
- In a world home to 6 billion people, roughly 600 million e-mails are sent every 10 minutes.
- E-mail is changing the way we read and communicate.
- 77 percent of workers report that e-mail downtime causes major stress at work, with 10 percent actually assaulting their computers.
- As a result, some psychologists are actually pushing to have "Internet Addiction" broadly classified as a clinical disorder. (136)

But Freeman isn't the only media prophet warning us about the impact of technological disruption. In his blog (http://socialnomics.net/) based on the book *Socialnomics*, Erik Qualman lists mind-boggling statistics about how social media has impacted our culture:

- In 2010, Generation Y outnumbered Baby Boomers . . . 96 percent of them have already joined a social network.
- One out of eight couples married in the United States in the last year met via social media.
- If Facebook were a country, it would be the world's third largest, between the United States and India.
- A 2009 U.S. Department of Education study revealed that, on average, online students outperformed those receiving face-to-face instruction. One in six higher education students is enrolled in online curriculum.
- The fastest-growing segment on Facebook is 55-to-65-year-old females.
- Ashton Kutcher and Ellen Degeneres (combined) have more Twitter followers than the populations of Ireland, Norway, or Panama.

- Generation Y and Z consider e-mail passé . . . In 2009, Boston College stopped distributing e-mail addresses to incoming freshmen.
- There are more than 200,000,000 blogs—increasing daily and 54 percent of bloggers post content or tweet daily. Because of the speed in which social media enables communication, word of mouth now becomes world of mouth.
- 78 percent of consumers trust peer recommendations, but only 14 percent trust advertisements.
- 25 percent of Americans in the past month said they watched a short video . . . on their phone.
- In the near future we will no longer search for products and services, they will find us via social media.

At the start of 2010, marketing expert Seth Godin called the upcoming ten years the decade of change and frustration. As Seth elaborated on his online blog:

Change: The infrastructure of massive connection is now real. People around the world have cell phones. The first Internet generation is old enough to spend money, go to work, and build companies. Industries are being built every day (and old ones are fading). The revolution is in full swing, and an entire generation is eager to change everything because of it. Hint: it won't look like the last one with a few bells and whistles added.

Frustration: Baby boomers are getting old. Dreams are fading, and so is health. Boomers love to whine, and we love to imagine that we'll live forever and accomplish everything. This is the decade that reality kicks in. And, to top it off, savings are thin and resource availability isn't what it used to be. A lot of people ate their emergency rations during the last decade. Look for this frustration to be acted out in public, and often. (http://sethgodin.typepad.com/)

In so many ways, media and technology have overtaken our lives, and along with great benefits, they have also brought great frustration. We can't escape the advertisements from video monitors embedded in gas pumps and elevators. We used to fear "billboard jungles" in major cities, but today, technology is allowing companies to target us far more effectively—often without our even realizing it's happened. In fact, some researchers indicate that we're being exposed to the phenomenal number of five thousand media messages per person, per day.

That barrage is impacting our behavior. For instance, people answer mobile phones in the most inappropriate places. My wife, Kathleen, and I attended a wedding recently where a member of the audience refused to take off his wireless Bluetooth earpiece. As the church lights dimmed for the wedding procession, he sat there with the little blue light blinking away in his ear like some cheap disco ball. I wondered what phone call could be so important that he couldn't even take off his earpiece for the bride's entrance.

Our close friend Fred Applegate is a respected musical theater performer in major roles on Broadway in shows like *The Sound of Music*, *The Producers*, and *Young Frankenstein*. One night during a performance, the cast was interrupted by a cell phone ringing in the audience. To the astonishment of everyone in the theater, the patron actually took the call! The actors paused onstage to hear the audience member say in a loud voice: "Hello? No, I can't talk. I'm at a Broadway show."

> » **THE INVASION OF TECHNOLOGY—ESPECIALLY IN THE HANDS OF STUPID PEOPLE—IS A HORRIFYING THOUGHT INDEED.**

But it's more than technology that's changing. As I write this, we're experiencing a major financial recession. As a result, most people are cutting back financially in key areas to weather the storm. But according to a recent poll, 32 percent of respondents said they're spending less *across the board*. More telling, however, is that these consumers expect this cutback to be their "new normal pattern" for the future. One study found that 75 percent have altered their purchasing in the last year. While some have traded down, most seem to have evolved into a completely new lifestyle. Steve McClellan quoted David Kenny, an advertising agency executive: "People are going to emerge from the current recession forever changed."

» THE RECESSION IS NOW, BUT DISRUPTION IS THE "NEW NORMAL."

That's why it's so critical for all of us to master the principles that will allow us to survive *and thrive* in the culture of disruption that is rapidly becoming our future.

I'm a writer, filmmaker, and media producer, and I started my career directing television programs. I'm a cofounder of a television production company in Los Angeles, as well as a company that focuses on helping nonprofit organizations use the media more effectively. I'm not a doomsayer. I'm an enthusiastic media user and probably value my iPhone, iPad, and laptop as much as anyone. But the truth is, we're living in the midst of the greatest shift in our culture since the invention of the printing press. And it's not the calm eye of a hurricane; it's the heart of the storm—the belly of the beast. As I write this, America is experiencing one of the most serious recessions in its history, changes in technology are disrupting our lives, and cultural norms that have held true for millennia are eroding before our eyes. We're losing family, cultural, and religious frameworks that have stabilized and supported earlier generations.

NAVIGATING THE WORLD OF DISRUPTIVE CHANGE

Out of clutter, find simplicity. From discord, find harmony.
In the middle of difficulty lies opportunity.
—ALBERT EINSTEIN

How do we choose to deal with these radical changes in our culture and in our lives? Do we follow the Luddites, who in early-nineteenth-century Britain rebelled against mechanizing the textile industry by destroying looms they felt were leaving them without work and changing their entire way of life? Or do we just let go and allow technology to overtake us in a wave and wash us away like a boat with no rudder?

You probably have examples of both camps right in your own neighborhood or your company. Some think an answering machine is radical technology and still refuse to use a computer. I have a pastor friend who won't buy a mobile phone, fearing both the loss of personal space and the ability to find privacy in a cluttered world. On the other extreme, I have close friends who are "gadget addicted." They have standing orders for the latest wide-screen TV, mobile device, or computer. They scan the Internet daily for the *next big thing*.

I'm not crazy about either approach, and that's why this book is about a third way.

> » I BELIEVE IT'S POSSIBLE TO
> NAVIGATE THE CULTURAL SHIFT
> WITHOUT LOSING YOUR SOUL.

We don't have to trade our freedom for connectivity, our values for financial success, or our devotion to God for our commitment to technology. Perhaps more important, we can actually embrace this radical disruption and make it work for us.

The secret is understanding the power of change.

> *There is comfort in chaos.*
> —JEREMY GUTSCHE, *EXPLOITING CHAOS*

A "jolt" is a shock, a disturbance, an abrupt change. It shakes things up and realigns our thinking. Like the Reset button on a computer, it cleans out the clutter that was slowing us down and allows us to start fresh.

In today's world of overwhelming disruption, if we can understand the power of change and how to make it work for us, it will allow us to take back the control of our lives. We can make the right choices, rather than having choices forced on us.

> » EITHER WE TAKE BACK CONTROL, OR WE'LL SPEND
> THE REST OF OUR LIVES AT THE MERCY OF OTHER
> PEOPLE WHO WILL DO IT FOR US.

The truth is, we all have things we want to change—we'd like to make more money, advance in our careers, find a husband or wife, turn the company around, become better leaders, have a better education, live in a different place, change our perspectives on living, change the dynamics of our marriages, find God, stop smoking or drinking, lose weight, get in shape, and more. The dream that we can change our lives is always out there, lurking behind the growing speed of our day-to-day living.

On the other hand, change is sometimes thrust upon us. We're often forced to change, but we're just not ready. Maybe you have been fired or laid off or passed over for a promotion; perhaps you can't sell your dream project, your spouse has left you, or the fire has gone out of your marriage; possibly you have a serious health problem, are losing your business, or just can't find a good reason to go on living. When change is forced on you, you have to respond with—you guessed it—more change.

Everyone needs to change something. The problem is, *we just don't know how.*

Our bosses, boards of directors, spouses, doctors, friends, and even our pastors, priests, or rabbis all tell us we need to change. Sometimes they can even get us excited about the possibilities and make us genuinely want to change. But when the excitement wears off, we're back to the same place all over again.

> *How do we actually change our lives?*
> *What are the steps we need to take to make a difference and start*
> *   over again?*
> *How do we get from where we are to where we want to be?*

That's what this book is about. I'm not interested in getting you "amped up," excited, or in a frenzy to change. Lots of books can do that—but when the excitement is over, you're left in the same rut as before.

This book is different from anything you've ever read. I'm going to show you step-by-step how to change your life or your organization (or both) in the context of today's disrupted world. It's far more than a simplistic self-help book, but on the other hand it's not a complex business book filled with jargon, diagrams, and intricate strategies that only a PhD could understand. The bottom line is that whatever the problem, challenge, or obstacle you face—or how chaotic or overwhelming your life may be—I believe the unique approach in this book will help you take the concrete steps to jolt your life and make real change happen.

Stop focusing on the problem and start focusing on the change.

Once it happens to you, it can happen to everyone around you. Thirty years of making change happen in organizations across America has taught me that *companies and organizations don't change until people change.*

> » YOU DON'T CHANGE *ORGANIZATIONS*
> WITHOUT CHANGING *PEOPLE.*

It's never too late to be who you might have been.
—GEORGE ELIOT, AUTHOR

I work in the media industry, where I see many who originally dreamed of being writers, actors, directors, or producers discover the difficulty of making those dreams come true. In Los Angeles, sometimes it seems as if every waiter, bookstore clerk, or bank teller is really an actor looking for his or her big break.

The truth is, people from all walks of life are desperate for change. When Henry David Thoreau wrote, "The mass of men lead lives of quiet desperation," he was talking about the difficult search for change and the sad truth that most people have simply given up on the possibility.

You must be the change you wish to see in the world.
—MAHATMA GANDHI

I've spent my career working with organizations that have hit a wall. I get the call when their product sales are flat, audience response has fallen, or their markets have evolved. But it took me years to discover that my *real* calling is shaking up people's thinking and making change happen.

As a result, I become a "spark" or a "catalyst" that changes leaders' perspectives and, hopefully, transforms their approach to business. I help them through the difficult process of change, in order for them to stay competitive and keep up with evolving trends, customers, and audiences.

I've been doing this for decades, and early on I realized it wasn't an *organizational* problem—it was a *people* problem. Jeff Hawkins, the creator of the first

Palm handheld PDA, said, "Companies don't innovate, *people* do." Certainly many organizations have outdated policies, rules, and processes that need to be updated. For many, it has become a culture of monotony—the assumed way that employees are supposed to react, think, and process issues. But the fact is, all organizations are driven by people, and I've discovered that if you just look hard enough, you'll find those crazy policies, outdated rules, and cultural problems all began with a person, and it's people who continue to breed that type of thinking.

So I turned my focus away from the organizations themselves and more toward the people who lead them.

That research and study resulted in the journey that you're beginning. It can't be denied: *change is hard.*

It's difficult to do well, and it's even harder to develop a lifestyle of change. As I've developed this process, marketing teams, creative teams, and even church groups have worked through the process with amazing results.

Either way, if you can master these relatively simple techniques, you can discover the infinite promise that change can bring into your life and into your organization.

It's time to look forward.

As Leonard Sweet said in *SoulTsunami: Sink or Swim in New Millennium Culture*: "The Dick-and-Jane world of my '50's childhood is over, washed away by a tsunami of change. Some technologies function as deluges that sweep all before it; some technologies are most like winter storms that swell the rivers of change. Electronics is the former. It has created a sea change such as the world has never experienced before"(17).

Leonard Sweet was right. A revolution of change is not only moving forward, but it is gaining momentum. Talking backstage at a national conference years ago, I proudly told him that our generation grew up writing letters, but we've recognized the need to change, so we switched to e-mail. But he laughed and reminded me of our children, who believe e-mail is far too old-fashioned (it's really just an electronic version of a letter) and not "instant" enough for a new generation.

Change never stops.

THE CRIPPLING POWER OF DENIAL

What is now proved was once impossible.
—WILLIAM BLAKE, POET

What do most people do in the face of disruption and chaos?

Most ignore it. You have no idea how many people I've counseled and consulted with who refuse to face the fact that change is happening and transforming the way we do everything. These people have a remarkable ability to deny the truth and ignore what's happening in the world around them. They actually do exist, and I've discovered most are miserable people—having exchanged the unknown for a life of monotony, sameness, and boredom.

But America will never again be the picket-fence culture of the fifties. Business, religion, media, politics, values, morality, and even family have all changed. The debate over whether those changes have been good or bad is another book, but what's most important now is that we realize *change has happened and this culture is never going back.*

BORN INTO CHANGE

My family has always been a long line of people who hated change. Born in a small mill town in rural North Carolina, I experienced firsthand how people can build an entire life without the slightest variation. For generations, my family all worked at a cotton mill, making sheets and towels. For her entire working life, my aunt worked in what they called the "sheet room," folding and packaging bedsheets. My uncle worked in the "towel room" doing pretty much the exact same things with towels. The thought of moving to a different position never crossed their minds, and they literally held the same positions from the time they started their jobs after high school until they retired, decades later.

My family loved uniformity. They would eat at the same restaurants, order the same food, attend the same church, and go to the same place every year on vacation. Working at the cotton mill was their existence, and nothing ever changed.

At least until my father was born.

Billy Cooke was a high school football star. A great athlete with an inquisitive nature, after graduation my dad lasted about a week at the mill. On his first day at the job, they gave him a big canvas hamper on wheels and had him push it from department to department, picking up all the irregular sheets and towels.

Pushing that hamper one time around the mill was enough to tell him that life was more than sheets and towels. When the horn went off at the end of the shift, my father headed straight for the United States Marines recruiting office, where he signed up to be a soldier.

He wanted out, and he knew the only way to change his life was to get as far away from the mill as he could.

His family was shocked. World War II had just been declared, and it was certain that after his basic training, my father would be sent to the Pacific to fight the Japanese. But looking back, I believe the shock came more from his decision to walk away from the mill and its predictable lifestyle than from his joining the Marines. What about the regular paycheck? What about the benefits? No one walks away from life at the mill!

Talk about a jolt. My father joined the Marines, was assigned to the legendary First Marine Division, hit the beaches at Guadalcanal and other hot spots in the Pacific, and became a local hero—sending dispatches from the war back for a column in the community newspaper. Looking back, I imagine the only time he ever had second thoughts about going back to the mill was when he was frantically digging a foxhole under heavy enemy fire.

After the war, he became our first family member to graduate from college. Then he attended seminary, became a voracious reader who had a personal library of more than five thousand volumes, received his PhD in theology, and became a successful pastor who founded and led numerous churches from North Carolina to Oklahoma.

My father learned to love change.

Occasionally I could see the tug of the "mill life" pulling at my dad. For instance, he loved to stay at a tacky, turquoise-colored hotel at the beach every summer, and it took us years to break him of that habit. In his later years, he had a thing for eating at restaurants where they have pictures of the food on the menus. But those little habits were nothing compared to the major life change of breaking from his past, having a vision for a new life, and pursuing that goal to the end.

As a child, watching my father instilled in me a vision for change. My father discovered more direction and purpose for his life than any member of our family had ever done. We were also better off financially, and both my sister and I graduated from college. I followed in my father's footsteps and earned my PhD and have been a change agent for millions of people through my work in television and the media. No one could have imagined the impact that one single decision my father made to leave the mill would have on his life and the lives of millions of others.

In the same way, you have no idea how making a positive decision to jolt your thinking will impact you, your employees, associates, friends and family, and potentially millions of people you've never even met. Like ripples in a pond, a single changed life reverberates in ways you could never dream of and touches lives for generations to come.

Before you continue, make the same decision my father made after his first grueling day on the job at the mill, then standing, sweating in the heat of that small-town military recruiting office. As he signed his name to the bottom of that government form, he realized turning back was not an option.

It was time for a jolt.

WHY JOLT!?

You may wonder why I use the term *jolt* to describe these changes. I use *jolt* because real change is big. It's a commitment. To initiate lasting, powerful change in our lives, we need to make a decision and shake up our complacent thinking. It's about facing the subjects we refuse to discuss and challenging our preconceived notions about the world around us.

» **IT'S ABOUT NOT JUST POINTING OUT THE ELEPHANT IN THE ROOM, BUT ABOUT POINTING OUT THE ELEPHANTS IN OUR LIVES.**

In many ways this book isn't about knowing the future; it's about being ready for the future. It's not about having the right *answers*; it's about asking the right *questions*. And it's not about things that seem *urgent*; it's about the things that *matter*.

Artist Andy Warhol once said, "They always say time changes things, but you actually have to change them yourself."

This isn't about waiting for change or expecting someone else to do the changing. It's about navigating changes in the world that will result in a new perspective on living, a better understanding of the world around you, the ability to recognize new opportunities, and a stronger vision for the future.

I believe you have enormous potential. But if you're ever going to achieve that potential, you need to jolt your thinking, understand the power of change, and discover how to achieve long-lasting, revolutionary transformation in every area of your life.

JOLT
YOUR
DIRECTION

THE TIME TO CHANGE IS NOW

Let the Revolution Begin!

Only I can change my life. No one can do it for me.
—CAROL BURNETT

I never realized how important the "now" of living was until I was fired from my job when I was thirty-six.

I had been working for a number of years at a media organization in the Midwest, when the president decided it was time for me to move on. I had been thinking about leaving for some time and had even booked a ticket to Los Angeles to see about the possibilities on the West Coast, but being fired always takes you by surprise. It was quick, clean, and efficient.

I'll never forget telling my wife, Kathleen. We had been married about twelve years, and although we had always dreamed about moving to Los Angeles and working in the media and entertainment industries there, it's amazing how you buy a home, have a couple of kids, get locked into your friends, and before long the dream has been replaced by the reality of everyday living.

The older you get, the harder change becomes.

We kept putting the dream on the shelf, intoxicated by the drug of a regular paycheck and a mortgage. But now, that life was over. And the slow, thoughtful transition that I had planned for moving to Los Angeles was replaced by a real jolt—the need to make a decision *now*.

Looking back, it was the best thing that could have possibly happened to me. I had been lulled into thinking that perhaps this was my future and perhaps "settling" for less than my dream was the right thing to do.

3

> *Great businesses have a point of view, not just a product or service.*
> *You have to believe in something. You need to have a backbone.*
> *You need to know what you're willing to fight for.*
> —JASON FRIED AND DAVID HEINEMEIER HANSSON, *REWORK*

This book is about one central theme: *how to live your life successfully against the backdrop of dramatic change and disruption.* In today's chaotic world, nothing stays the same. Assuming that your life today will continue uninterrupted is simply a recipe for disaster.

There's a wonderful scene in the Jason Reitman movie *Up in the Air*, starring George Clooney. Clooney plays Ryan Bingham, whose unusual job is to fire people from theirs. He's hired by major corporations to handle big layoffs. Although he's become brilliant at the task, the anguish, hostility, and despair of the job have left him empty, falsely compassionate, and yet—strangely—loving every second of it. In a powerful scene where he and a new assistant are firing an aging middle manager, Clooney notices on the manager's résumé that he had been trained as a French chef. As the manager despairs over losing his job and having to face his wife and kids, Clooney reminds him of his original dream. He asks a remarkable question, the essence of which is, *"Back when you started, how much did it take to buy you away from your dream?"*

It is a compelling scene as the middle manager thinks back to the time he exchanged a steady paycheck for what he really wanted to do with his life. Now, decades later, he realizes the devastating impact of settling for second best.

Have you ever rationalized settling for second best? It's amazing how you can make it sound as if it's the right thing to do, even when your innermost being is crying out for you to follow your heart and discover your real potential.

It's a good job . . .
We have good benefits . . .
The kids are in good schools . . .
The church is very supportive . . .
The company is really growing . . .
I can't take a risk with my family right now . . .
All our friends are here . . .

We're close to where our family lives . . .
People tell me I'd be foolish to pack up and move away now . . .
I have a lot invested in our retirement account . . .

There are a million reasons and ways to rationalize keeping your life exactly the same, and I knew them all. I was slowly exchanging a dream for security and giving away my future for what I had convinced myself was the right thing to do.

But fortunately I had the benefit of a serious jolt—getting tossed out on the street. What I couldn't do for myself, someone else helped me do, and I will be forever grateful.

I didn't realize it at the time, but my life as a change agent was just beginning. I had always been creative, hated monotony, and loved change, but now it would become the single most important part of my life.

After Kathleen and I sat on the bed, cried a little, and realized that we were leaving our life in the Midwest behind, we immediately began focusing on what was next, and it was the beginning of one of the most exhilarating experiences of our lives.

First, we began to scale down. It's amazing what you collect after ten or more years of marriage. We had an attic full of stuff, a garage packed to the rafters, and more on the back porch. But we knew if we were to move to Los Angeles, we'd need to be lean and mean, so we had an immediate garage sale, gave some things away, and got our entire world down to a rental truck and trailer.

Next, we started networking. I knew that I had limited severance pay and would need all of that to help us move, so I needed some work and needed it quick. I started phoning everyone I knew in the industry, started e-mailing friends, widening the net. And it worked. An old friend at a major energy company gave me my first freelance assignment, and it began building from there.

We changed our priorities, our focus, our habits, and our thinking, and we were able to take a difficult situation and turn it from tragedy into triumph.

When asked about his secret for fabulous wealth, billionaire H. L. Hunt described it in a four-step formula:

1. Decide what you want.
2. Decide what you are willing to give up to get it.

3. Set your priorities accordingly.
4. Be about it!

How much did it take to buy you away from your dream? Whatever it was, the time to change is now. Make a commitment, take a stand, and be about it!

THE HEADACHE IS WORTH IT

The Joy of Hitting the Wall

Things do not change; we change.
—HENRY DAVID THOREAU

After I was fired, my wife and I began the greatest journey of change we had ever experienced, because I had hit a wall. I had no other choice. I had run out of options, and there was only one answer—change or die.

Perhaps you've hit your wall. Maybe you've been fired, divorced, financially ruined, or have hit bottom from substance abuse, been humiliated, scared, or had a close call with death. If your life has been completely turned upside down and you're at the end of your rope, then you have it easy.

That's right—*you have it easy!*

When you change direction in life, the most difficult aspect of the change process is beginning. Taking the first step. Just as I did, most people will rest on their laurels, take the easy way out, rationalize their options, sacrifice their future, or diminish their past—anything—to keep from changing. If you've hit your wall and have no other options, then your decision is already made. Your choice has been decided and you're on the way up.

But if you haven't quite hit bottom yet and been jolted into reality, the choice is going to be much tougher. Your thoughts might include:

Sure I'm frustrated with my job, but at least it's a paycheck, and a lot of people are out of work right now.

7

Our sales aren't what I'd like them to be, but making a major company change right now would take some time.

Yeah, I wanted to be an actor, but moving to New York or Los Angeles would be a lot of work, and I'm not sure I really want to go back to living in a one-bedroom apartment again.

I'm not really drinking that much, and after all, I could really quit just about any time.

Oh, I dreamed about a different life, but that was a kid's dream. It's not really something that's realistic for me to pursue now.

There's no question that I could advance faster if I got my college degree, but I work all day, so why should I spend my evenings going to class?

I could go on and on. I don't know your particular frustration, but I'm sure you have a million excuses for why you've never begun your journey to change. You haven't hit your particular wall, so your life could easily go on for years, maybe your whole life, before you realize you've traded your dream for a shallow, empty copy.

» WHEN A GUN'S AT YOUR HEAD, YOU CAN'T AFFORD TO BE COMPLACENT.

If you're like most people, to begin the journey of change, you have to reach the place where you realize there is simply no other choice. But if you have the slightest frustration that perhaps your dream is dying, then that's all you need. There really are second chances in life, and this is yours. Don't wait until you hit bottom, get fired, gamble your life away, settle for a dead-end job, or lose your spouse to divorce. Don't wait until you're too old, too cranky, or too locked into your lifestyle.

In their book *Unleashing the Killer App*, Larry Downes and Chunka Mui described the Law of Disruption: "Social, economic, and legal systems change incrementally, but technology changes exponentially" (29). It's been said that every twelve to eighteen months, the processing power of computers doubles. Technology is changing every day, but people change incrementally—and some, not at all.

But when people won't change, circumstances have a powerful way of forcing the issue. As eighteenth-century poet, writer, and critic Samuel Johnson said: "Nothing focuses the mind like a hanging." More recently, former secretary of state Henry Kissinger translated it to: "The absence of alternatives clears the mind marvelously."

Foresight is a marvelous thing, but the truth is, as long as we see any other way out, very few of us will muster the will to make real change happen.

The music industry is filled with the ghosts of executives who didn't recognize online music downloading as a viable business. As I write this chapter, Amazon.com has announced that e-books have surpassed the sales of traditional hardbound volumes, and just like the music industry, book publishers who didn't recognize the shift are shutting their doors. Even some who *pioneer* change don't go quite far enough. (Remember the Sony Walkman?)

But the good news is, hitting a wall can be your ticket to freedom because it forces you to change course and to do it *now*.

A friend in the computer industry saw the wall coming. He could have denied reality (the way many do) and kept moving forward until he crashed. But he made the decision to hire two market researchers to figure out what was next in his business. Their answers encouraged him to shift markets, and today he's far more successful in a completely different field.

A client of mine thought he was doing great until doctors discovered he had developed cancer of the esophagus. His illness, treatment, and recovery forced him to leave his business and literally took him out of everything for more than four years. Thinking his career was over, he nearly gave up. But when a surprise recovery jolted him, he realized the experience had completely changed his perspective on life. As a result, he's transformed his thinking about his purpose for living, and it's catapulted him to an entirely new level of success.

Whatever your wall—getting fired, losing your home, receiving the medical diagnosis you've dreaded, closing your business, bankruptcy, whatever—it doesn't have to be the end. As terrible as the wall may be, you can overcome it if you use the moment to jolt you back to reality.

While transitions are admittedly uncomfortable and disruptive . . . job insecurity or loss can provide a life-changing jolt.
—BECKY BEAUPRE GILLESPIE AND HOLLEE SCHWARTZ TEMPLE, *ABA JOURNAL*

I have a distant family member who is an ocean-going captain of some of the largest oil tankers in the world. He pilots the behemoths from port to port, satisfying countries thirsty for oil. Early in my career, I produced a video presentation for a major oil company and was amazed at the sheer size of the vessels. Fully loaded, they sink deep into the ocean and take enormous power to propel forward. Over dinner one night my relative told me that it takes up to fifteen miles to turn a fully loaded tanker. In fact, they have to plan a turn at least twenty miles out because it's just so heavy it takes that long to make the change.

Hearing that fact made me realize that changing major companies, big labor unions, or any massive organization is nearly impossible unless people realize that jolt has to happen and it has to start *now*.

And that's exactly where you need to be. As long as there's a way out, a second chance, or another alternative, you'll never be committed enough to change. You have to face the fact that circumstances won't change until *you* change. Family members won't change until you change. Your job won't change until you change. And your future will never change until you make the decision to change.

Embrace the wall. Let it help you focus your mind and face the real truth about your situation.

But how do you face the truth? Sometimes, the key lies in your past.

THE REAL TRUTH
ABOUT CHANGE

Letting Go of Your Past

Disconnecting from change does not recapture the past. It loses the future.
—KATHLEEN NORRIS, WRITER

Keeping score of old scores and scars, getting even and one-upping, always make you less than you are.
—MALCOLM FORBES, PUBLISHER, *FORBES*

The third step toward jolting your life is to face the truth and let go of your past. Significant numbers of people never change their lives because they just can't let go of history. Some can't forgive people who abused them, cheated on them, lied to them, fired them, or more. Perhaps you suffered from childhood abuse and can't bring yourself to forgive and let it go. Perhaps you were cheated financially or experienced business failure and refuse to get past the experience. Perhaps you discovered something as an adult about your parents or spouse that has changed your perspective of your family.

Perhaps it's not being cheated or abused by others; it could be your own personal failures. I recently spoke to a large business gathering in Los Angeles, composed of leaders from a wide range of companies. During my talk the audience wrote questions on index cards for me to answer at the end of the event. The single most asked question was: *How can I overcome a failure from my past and be successful again?*

That seminar taught me just how many people live under the bondage of past failure.

Whatever your particular experience, you can't feed it, ignore it, or deny it. You have to forgive and let it go. Ultimately, when you refuse to forgive—for any reason—it only hurts you. Someone said that not being able to forgive is like taking poison and expecting the other person to die. I've had things stolen from me, money cheated from our company, lies told about me, and more, but it didn't take much to realize the longer I focused on it, the more bitter I became.

> » IN THE DIGITAL AGE,
>   YOU CAN'T HIDE FAILURE.

Google isn't just about *search*, it's about reputation management. The river of information that flows online is a tsunami, and whatever failure you've experienced in your past will show up in a Google search. So get used to it. Today we need to embrace our pasts and live more transparent lives than ever. Even more important, *we need to stop looking in the rearview mirror and instead concentrate on the road ahead.*

I know one pastor who early in his career was forced out of a church because a leading church member felt the pastor had slighted him. It was an insignificant and completely innocent act on the part of the pastor, but the petty church member was enraged and used his influence in the church to have the board eventually dismiss the pastor. It was wrong, but the pastor was booted out of a church he had invested years into and had built from obscurity to being one of the leading churches in the city.

It was a difficult and embarrassing time for the young pastor, so much so that he could not bring himself to forgive that church member or the church board. Everywhere he went he talked about how he had been cheated. He brought it up at family gatherings, business meetings, and other events. After a while, people got tired of hearing about it. It was consuming the pastor's life. He pastored other churches, but they soon tired of his unrelenting stories of how the previous church had cheated him and tried to destroy his ministry. Before long, churches stopped interviewing him because he simply would not let up. Bitterness controlled every aspect of his life.

Eventually he retired, never having accomplished his potential in the pulpit. His ministry was crippled, and his life came to very little because he refused to forgive. In essence, the pastor had not only been cheated by that church member years before, but worse, had allowed the church member's act—however wrong—to control the rest of his life.

Which is worse? Suffering abuse at the hands of someone in the past or allowing that incident to destroy the rest of your life?

In order to move forward, you have to let go and be at peace with your past.

Some think it's holding on that makes one strong; sometimes it's letting go.
—SYLVIA ROBINSON, VOCALIST

Is it hard? Of course it is. It may be one of the most difficult things you'll have to do in your life.

At the *Apollo One* monument at Cape Canaveral, Florida, there's an inscription that reads: *Ad astra per aspera.* Translated, it means: "A rough road leads to the stars."

Sometimes I think reaching the moon is a piece of cake compared to the difficulty some people have with change.

THE FOUR KEYS TO MOVING ON

In my experience, there are four important keys to getting past your hurt, brokenness, and failure and moving forward. Throughout the book we'll discuss each in detail.

Key #1: Realize the benefit.

Once you face what happened and acknowledge the damage it's cost your life, you have to *realize the incredible benefit of forgiving the offender(s) and moving on with your life.* Letting it go and looking forward will allow you to focus on the future and begin making positive changes in your life.

Key #2: Learn to live with ambiguity.

There are no easy answers. If there were, life would be great, we'd never face any challenges, and the future would be rosy. To change means to face things we've never seen, visit places we've never visited, and encounter the unknown. It means a spiritual quest as much as an intellectual one.

But most people prefer easy answers. Just visit a typical bookstore and check out the self-help section. The shelves are filled with titles that feature easy steps to financial achievement, trouble-free keys to success, and simple strategies for health, wellness, and fulfillment in life. Most business and even religious books aren't much different.

But life is hard. And somewhere deep inside, you know that all those simplistic approaches to life just don't work—especially for the long haul.

> » **SUCCESS IN LIFE IS MORE ABOUT ASKING THE RIGHT QUESTIONS AND MAKING THE TOUGH JOURNEY.**

Don't feel that just because life is difficult, you're not on the right path. An old Southern preacher said, "If you don't come face-to-face with the devil sometimes, then you must be going the same direction he is."

Key #3: Expect to lose some friends.

The moment your life starts to change, someone—somewhere—won't like it. Chances are, some of your closest friends are people who will never change and don't like people who do. Your decision to change doesn't mean others around you will do the same. But you have to be committed to growing, expanding your knowledge and experience, and moving to the next level in life. I've discovered that when some of your friends decide against making the journey, you'll be more than compensated by others you'll meet along the way—people who have the same interests and goals and who want to make a difference.

> » **LOVE YOUR FRIENDS AND RESPECT THEM, BUT NEVER ABANDON YOUR DREAMS BECAUSE YOUR FRIENDS LACK THE VISION TO JOIN YOU.**

Key #4: Start with a clean slate when it comes to "how."

Forget how you've done things in the past and open yourself up to new possibilities and ideas. It's amazing, but I still encounter the well-worn phrase

"But we've always done it this way." So many people are locked into old ways of thinking, tired methods, and useless techniques that it's almost impossible to get them to see the possibilities of the new.

I'm often brought into an organization facing serious challenges, only to be limited by their frustrating desire to continue old ways of thinking. The truth is, if the old way of thinking worked, why would they need me? And yet they persist in doing the same thing(s) in the same way(s) but wanting different results.

It's ultimately about insecurity, and I could write an entire book on that issue alone. I've discovered that when faced with the possibility of change or a new way of doing things, people react in two different ways. *Secure* people react with excitement and anticipation. But *insecure* people react with fear and hesitation. Insecure people are the ones who drag their feet, "forget" to do things they've been asked to do, subvert meetings, and figure out a million other ways to sabotage the process.

Perhaps you were told that you'd never make it, you don't have what it takes, or you'd never amount to anything. Whoever told you that had no idea of all your capabilities, because no one can know the full potential or the full range of possibilities in another human being, and no one can tell for certain where your limits are or how far you can reach.

You may believe in God or be an atheist or an agnostic. But I believe that you were born for a purpose. You were not a cosmic accident, and your life has not been a mistake. I believe that each of us has a purpose that only we can accomplish and a promise that each of us was born to fulfill.

Turbulence is life force. It is opportunity.
Let's love turbulence and use it for change.
—RAMSEY CLARK, FORMER ATTORNEY GENERAL

As you read this book, take control of your own story and stop letting fear control your life. You are not the result of random chance. You are here for a purpose, and you'll never experience real change until you discover it. Now it's time to start exploring that purpose and move to a new level of confidence.

START AT THE FINISH LINE

Knowing Your Dream and Destination

A sailor without a destination cannot hope for a favorable wind.

—LEON TEC, MD

Shortly after college, I led a team deep into the headwaters of the Amazon River to film the work of a medical team in a remote village deep in the rain forests of Brazil. I discovered that getting there wasn't easy or safe—in fact, the greatest challenge was finding out just where "there" was.

We flew commercially about halfway up the Amazon River and then chartered a small private plane. I'll never forget sitting on a beat-up oil drum in the back of the plane, which about midflight I discovered was filled with the fuel for the return trip! Between the weight of that fuel drum, our camera equipment, and the crew of four people, the small plane could barely take off. As we finally lifted off the ground, our right wheel clipped a tall tree at the end of the airstrip, and we all gave a huge sigh of relief as the plane veered upward toward the clouds.

It was an exhilarating trip following the Amazon River from the air, and after a few hours, we landed at a remote dirt airstrip in the jungle. We then boarded an old river freighter for another long day traveling even deeper into the rain forest. When the freighter could no longer navigate the narrow waterways near the source of the river, we loaded the film equipment onto small canoes and paddled for a day.

We finally arrived at our destination. The four of us had arrived at a place for which there were few maps, and what maps existed had little detail, markers, or points of reference.

And yet we made it.

We made it because I understood our destination. I didn't completely know how to get there, and our methods of transportation were unpredictable, plus once we started we had no outside communications. We didn't have many resources or much money. But we knew where we were going, and we understood when we arrived.

> » YOU CAN OVERCOME MANY OBSTACLES,
>   AS LONG AS YOU KNOW YOUR DESTINATION.

Having that singular goal made all the difference. The relationship of change to a specific destination is critical to understand.

We all had goals in our lives when we were children. But life has a way of distracting us from our early dreams, and few of us could actually say we've become what we dreamed as children. In my case, that's probably a good thing. Some research indicates that something significant happens to most people between the ages of five and seven. For some reason, creativity starts to drop at amazing speed. We start to believe that we aren't really that creative, and I believe that, as a result, our dreams and goals begin to die as well. It's interesting that right in the middle of that five-to-seven age range is one major life event—starting school. Is the switch from childhood "free-range" living and learning to one of disciplined, often rote learning responsible? I don't know. There are certainly convincing arguments on both sides of the issue. But it does tell me that, as parents, we certainly need to reinforce, encourage, and celebrate our children's creativity during those critical years.

But what's worse than giving up childhood dreams is that most adults lose the ability to dream at all. Somehow we believe the adult thing to do is to be grounded in reality, forget our daydreams, and settle for the hard realities of life.

There's no question that life can be hard. We all have mouths to feed, families to take care of, and house payments. But reality is a poor substitute for the ability to dream about the possibilities life has to offer and, even better, to actually experience the benefit of those dreams.

Goals in writing are dreams with deadlines.
—BRIAN TRACY, PERSONAL SUCCESS COACH

Whenever I feel my dreams losing steam, I always think of Booker T. Washington. Because he was born a slave, his childhood years were anything but pleasant. The family's farm cabin had no glass windows, and any opening to let in light also let in the freezing wind in the winter. The floor of the cabin was dirt. The life of a slave was backbreaking work that started before the sun came up and continued long after it went down again. Washington's childhood was also lived out during the Civil War, which created turmoil, fear, and uncertainty in the lives of Southern slaves and added additional pressure to an already hopeless state of affairs.

But in spite of that desperate situation, young Booker dreamed of an education. His goal was learning—real learning. Not just the ability to read a newspaper or dime-store novel, but a desire to learn science, mathematics, history, and more. Years later, working deep in a coal mine, he overheard some of the miners talking about a school five hundred miles away called the Hampton Institute. He immediately decided that one day he would attend the school, in spite of the distance.

His dream simply would not die. As a result, he not only attended the school but was later asked to lead a new program in Alabama, called the Tuskegee Institute. He eventually built Tuskegee into a major college campus with more than fifteen hundred students and a faculty of two hundred professors.

There was not one single thing in Booker T. Washington's life that helped him except the power of a dream. Starting out, he had no money, no education, no training, no influence, and no future. He was just another slave among thousands, with no potential other than living out his life working in obscurity on a forgotten Southern farm.

But the power of his dream opened doors, filled him with motivation, and revealed his true promise. Millions of Americans have been directly touched or indirectly inspired by his story, and this nation is a better place because he never gave up on his dream.

If you feel that your situation is hopeless, just remember Booker T. Washington and start dreaming again.

How do you do that? The key is to realize that goals are born in dreams, and dreams are simply the great what-ifs of life.

What if . . .

I could run a marathon?
we could make our marriage work?
we reorganized the company?
I went back to college?
I could write a novel?
we could double our sales?
I could get that promotion?
I could find the right career?
I could change my future?
I could be a better leader?
I could make a difference?

Goals are all about "what if," so begin thinking about the great what-ifs of your life. No limits, no lids. You're not a beauty pageant contestant, so I'm not necessarily looking for "world peace" here—I'm looking for goals that you personally dream about.

In the next chapter, we'll look at the keys for getting the right goals down on paper. A list will help clarify your life. For years you've thought about dreams and goals, but few people actually get them into a realistic list. This is the foundation for your life change because it will jolt you from dreaming to creating a map to your destination.

THE POWER OF "WHAT IF?"

Expanding Your Vision

Growth means change and change involves risk, stepping from the known to the unknown.
—GEORGE SHINN, PROFESSIONAL SPORTS FRANCHISE OWNER

The first stage of goal setting is the "blue sky" approach. Nothing is off-limits, out of bounds, or impossible—not one thing. This is your creative time, when you can dream about anything, and nothing is too strange or too crazy. Let yourself go, just as if you were that small child again, dreaming about what you'd be when you grew up.

I always encourage people to begin this way because as adults we get caught in too many hang-ups when it comes to our potential and possibilities. We put too many boundaries and restrictions on what we believe we can do. It's something that happens because of a lot of issues, like our misplaced idea of maturity, our education, or our perception that adulthood is about reality, restraint, and responsibility.

But this is your time to dream again. I recommend you start by finding a place where the phone won't ring, the TV is off, and the lure of e-mail or Facebook can't tempt you. You don't have to find a mountain cabin, but I do recommend you find a place that's relaxing and will put you in a creative mood.

Next, get a journal, or at least a blank piece of paper, and jot down some of your thoughts. Remember, write anything that comes to mind—goals to achieve and changes you want to make. Is your dream to be a barber or beekeeper? Real estate agent? Movie star? Store manager? Better mom? Game-show host? Company vice president? Screenwriter? College graduate? Stronger leader? Devoted father?

From a corporate perspective, you might want to double your sales, increase the staff, become number one in the marketplace, or rethink your global strategy.

Write it down. What about becoming an Olympic athlete? Put it on the paper. Think of any goal that might come to mind. New house? New city? New wardrobe?

And don't limit yourself to words. If drawing or even scribbling works better for you, then by all means do it. There are no rules or limitations here. Our purpose for the session is to get down your immediate thoughts, goals for your life, and areas you want to change. You don't have to be terribly specific either. This is big-picture time, and I'm more interested in the first thoughts and ideas that come into your head.

This is an occasion to expand your vision and stretch the muscles of your imagination. Millions of people are trapped in a self-imposed prison. They believe they aren't good enough, talented enough, or smart enough to accomplish much in life and are resigned to spending the rest of their days settling for second best. As a result, they limit their dreams and live within the borders of a second-class world.

> » **"DARE TO DREAM" IS AN OVERUSED PHRASE, BUT I ENCOURAGE YOU TO DO IT.**

The only real limitations in your life are in your mind, so break those shackles and look for a farther horizon. Write it down and don't let your past, other people's opinions, or the limitations of your experience hold you back.

It's important that you do this exercise a number of times. In fact, I recommend this become a regular creative workout. It will open up your thinking to new possibilities and force you to question all the old assumptions that have kept you from considering new options and choices.

I use this type of thinking in solving numerous problems and frustrations in my own life. Whether I have a challenge at work, in my family, or elsewhere, my first step is to look for solutions without any rules, restrictions, or boundaries. Forget reality for a moment and start thinking of potential options and choices out of the blue. Don't worry about budget, time limits, schedule, or whatever has or hasn't been done in the past.

Some of my students and clients consider this a waste of time. "But we have realistic budgets and time schedules," they moan. "What about company policies?" they plead. "We have to figure our company limitations into the solution."

Not at this point. This is the place where anything could happen and we start with a blank slate.

Why? Because this is where the most innovative solutions come from. You don't solve existing problems with existing rules. To do something new, you can't keep doing something old. Thinking in old ways will never solve new problems. You'll never be innovative unless you start with the greatest number of possibilities. Of course, many of your ideas won't work, but you'll never know unless you write them down and address them.

And you'll discover that very often the most creative and unusual solution will jump right out of that list, and it will be a solution that never would have been considered by someone whose thinking was restricted and bound.

So get your goals down first. Anything, everything, whatever you can think of or want to accomplish.

NARROW YOUR FOCUS

The reason most people never reach their goals is that they don't define them, or ever seriously consider them as believable or achievable.
Winners can tell you where they are going, what they plan to do along the way, and who will be sharing the adventure with them.
—DENIS WAITLEY, MOTIVATIONAL SPEAKER AND AUTHOR

After a few of these blue-sky sessions, you should have a list of interesting possibilities about where you want to go with your life and issues you want to change. Keep these notes because you'll find yourself coming back to the list from time to time.

Start by exploring the possibilities from the list and begin focusing on the goals that match your personality, gifts, and passion.

> » **FIRST, LOOK THROUGH THE LIST AND TOSS OUT GOALS OR CHANGES THAT SIMPLY CAN'T HAPPEN.**

For instance, if you're fifty years old, chances are you've missed your chance for an Olympic gold medal. It was a good dream, but that one's out of reach. Perhaps you can get a job working with the U.S. Olympic Committee or help mentor or train a local athlete, but short of a miracle, your competing is pretty much out of the question.

Other goals might be unattainable for a variety of reasons, such as geography, finances, or education. Don't toss those out yet, because you never know what can be achieved with a little creativity and someone determined to change. (Remember Booker T. Washington.)

> » **THE NEXT STEP IS TO SPEND TIME THINKING ABOUT YOUR GOALS IN TERMS OF YOUR PERSONAL GIFTS, TALENTS, PASSION, AND WILLINGNESS TO SACRIFICE.**

Nearly every week, I meet people who spend enormous amounts of money and time dreaming of a career they simply don't have the talent or ability to do well. All the passion and desire in the world will not make me a successful NBA walk-on or Super Bowl MVP. At some point, we have to realize the limitations of our abilities and not continue wasting our lives in the pursuit of an impossible goal.

On the other hand, there are millions of people with lofty goals who have simply not made the commitment it takes to achieve them. Being in the entertainment business, I am constantly meeting people who have written screenplays, and I usually have a stack of scripts on the edge of my desk. To be honest, 90 percent of the scripts are simply awful pieces of writing. Many producers and studio executives use the "ten-page rule" in reading these screenplays: if it doesn't capture our attention or impress us with compelling writing within ten pages, it hits the trash.

Many of these writers have great passion for their work and have sometimes put years into the process. I often get very emotional and passionate cover letters from writers who believe very strongly in their potential. Some believe they have an almost divine purpose in writing and desperately cling to the hope that a producer will eventually see the brilliance in their scripts and give them a shot.

While passion and desire are important, so are training, education, and preparation. Far too often I find writers who tell me they just don't have time to take classes or work with a writing teacher. They're convinced passion is all they need to become successful.

» **WOULD YOU HAVE BRAIN SURGERY BY A DOCTOR WHO HAD GREAT PASSION FOR HIS WORK BUT WHO DIDN'T HAVE THE TIME TO ATTEND MEDICAL SCHOOL?**

I doubt it. In the same way, we have to realize the importance of laying the groundwork and building the right foundation to make our goals and dreams happen.

Perhaps that's a change you need to make right now. Maybe your dreams have been frustrated because you haven't made the commitment of preparation. Want to be a pastor? Enroll in seminary. Want to be a doctor? Head to medical school. Want to be an architect? Get the training. Find an internship, volunteer, or develop a mentor relationship with someone with expertise in the area you want to pursue.

We'll discuss this in a later chapter on personal growth, but for now, I urge you to put in the preparation it will take to achieve your goal. Penicillin wasn't the culmination of a vast research project, it was the result of an accidental discovery. But it never would have happened had those scientists not had very definite goals in mind.

Chance favors only the prepared mind.
—LOUIS PASTEUR

You are different from every other person on the earth, and there are abilities and talents you were born with that will help determine your ultimate career, goal, or calling.

I'll use the word *calling* from time to time, which means "a sense of destiny and spiritual purpose." In the Christian sense, it means that God has called you for a specific purpose and that divine purpose is your reason for being. People of different faith perspectives have similar feelings about this area, and it's something I recommend you explore further. Some people have a calling to help inner-city children, some feel called to expand medical care to needy countries, and others feel called into the ministry.

A calling is the highest form of life purpose because it transcends the need for fame, financial success, or status. Calling drove Mother Teresa into the slums of Calcutta, compelled writer and Harvard professor Henri Nouwen to spend his life with the mentally handicapped and physically disabled, and persuaded Dr. Paul Brand to give up a prosperous medical practice to spend his life caring for lepers.

In a world absorbed in the reckless pursuit of riches and fame, you could do no better than experience a calling that would cause you to make a genuine difference in the world.

MOVING FROM THE GENERAL TO THE SPECIFIC

Now that you have a list of possibilities and are starting to narrow down those possibilities, it's time to focus on specific destinations. Start matching your goals to your own personal gifts and talents. Take a serious look where the match is the strongest.

First, a word about skills, gifts, and talents. People often have enormous difficulty determining what they are really good at doing. It should be quite easy, but many people spend their lives without thinking about their talents and therefore lose touch with their greatest strengths.

What do you find easy? Are you an exceptional leader? Do you make friends easily? Do you love numbers? What about financial advice, networking, decision-making skills, or managing in a crisis?

Draw two columns on your paper. List your goals on one side and your skills on the other. Don't be shy—this is the time to focus on your strengths, not to be modest.

There are formal evaluations that indicate personality types as well as strengths and weaknesses, such as the Myers-Briggs evaluation and the DISC profile. Some resources are low-cost or even free on the Internet—an example is Tom Rath's *Strengths Finder*. But if you don't have access to a professional evaluation, talk to some friends you respect and ask their advice. Show them the list of skills and talents you feel you possess, and get their feedback. Sometimes others see things you can't see, and might point out additional areas of strength.

Then, begin connecting potential dreams and goals to the appropriate skills and talents you possess.

Karen was raised in an environment where people told her she would never achieve anything significant. She was never encouraged or allowed to excel in anything and grew up believing she was worthless. She was an excellent math student in school, but her parents never paid any attention to it. It never crossed her mind that math was something that would help her beyond high school. Right out of school, she married a man who was no different from her parents, and she spent the next seven years being berated, criticized, and humiliated. When he unexpectedly died of an undiagnosed heart problem, she was forced into the job market, having no idea which direction to go or what career to pursue.

She tried a series of jobs—housekeeping, retail clerk, and factory worker—but was miserable at each position. One day at the factory, she was having lunch with an assistant bookkeeper who mentioned how far behind she was with the latest sales figures. Karen offered to help after work, and the minute she started adding up the figures, a light came on. She suddenly remembered her gift for math and plunged into the task with an excitement that amazed her friend. Karen finished in half the time it took her bookkeeper friend and so impressed the factory manager that he offered Karen a job in the accounting department.

Today the company is paying Karen to take night classes toward an accounting degree. For the first time in her life she feels as if she has a purpose. She loves her job and can't wait to get to work each day. The possibilities are wide-open for Karen. Because she decided to make the necessary changes in her life to go back to school and finish her degree, she will have the credentials to move into accounting, engineering, or anywhere else her passion for numbers can take her.

It's about connecting the dots, so stop dreaming and start connecting. Take your list of skills, gifts, and talents, and start connecting them to your dreams and goals.

The next step is to decide what really matters.

REVIEW
Jolt Your Direction

The time to change is now. List anything that is stopping you from making changes in your life today. Then answer the following questions.

1. What changes in my life need to be made?
2. Are there areas in my past I need to leave behind?
3. Do I need to forgive anyone in order to move forward with my life?
4. What is my destination?
5. At the end of the change process, what type of person will I be?
6. As a result of this book, what three major goals do I want to set for my life, and/or what three major changes do I want to make?

JOLT
WHAT
MATTERS

JOLT YOUR PRIORITIES

Taking Control of What Is Important

We do not have a money problem in America. We have a values and priorities problem.
—MARIAN WRIGHT EDELMAN, FOUNDER OF THE CHILDREN'S DEFENSE FUND

If your agenda is set by someone else and it doesn't lead you where you want to go, why is it your agenda?
—SETH GODIN, *LYNCHPIN*

Today we live in an oddly conflicted world, with a confused moral map. On the positive side, I bought a cup of coffee this morning from a national coffee chain that donates a portion of every sale to help the rain forest. My wife buys groceries at a store that only sells food produced in ways that help the environment. Office supply stores feature recycled paper, printer companies recondition print cartridges, and even mechanics now dispose of oil and grease in ways friendly to the environment.

All is well in the world.

On the other hand, in the age of Bernard Madoff, corporate corruption seems to be at an all-time high, the public trust of religious, media, and political leaders at an all-time low, and cheating on university campuses is almost becoming commonplace.

Even Martha Stewart did hard time.

OUR INTEGRITY NEEDS A JOLT

For an earlier generation, criteria for morality and behavior were pretty standard. There was a common moral framework in America, and it wasn't difficult to see where people stood. My dad was a pastor, and even people who never darkened the door of a church respected him and what he represented. In those days we didn't need movie ratings, we never had to view sex or profanity on television, and parents rarely worried about the safety of their children at school.

Certainly, there were distortions. Ricky and Lucy Ricardo slept in separate beds, even though they were married, and June Cleaver always cleaned house in high heels and a dress.

As a result of those types of distortions, the disillusionment of the sixties, and a cultural drive to break free of restraint, we plunged headlong into a moral chasm with little knowledge of where we would land. Yes, perhaps things are more relaxed and tolerant now, but we've paid a high price for the journey. Today we live in a world where children can access hard-core pornography at the touch of a computer keyboard, schools are rife with violence, and saying a prayer in class can get you suspended from school.

This book isn't an exploration of our national morality, but we do need to recognize how much the culture has changed in the last fifty years and understand the importance of moral courage.

I define moral courage as a set of personal principles you live by that are unchanging. Some people would call them moral absolutes, but however you choose to name them, they help create a life of moral purpose. Without moral purpose you will never reach your full potential.

> *The only true happiness comes from squandering ourselves for a purpose.*
> —WILLIAM COWPER, POET AND HYMN WRITER

In another generation, moral courage would be discussed only in religious terms, but today even secular corporations are embracing the concept. I believe it's because after fifty years of moral drift in this country, we are just beginning to see the damage from the pursuit of unchecked sexual freedom, rampant cheating, and a culture of "me first." Check out the self-help section of the average bookstore and note how many titles focus on *me*. What's in it for *me*, what do *I* get out of it, and do unto others before they do unto *me*.

Jonathan Last, in the *Weekly Standard* magazine, noted the impact of the Internet itself on the culture of narcissism when he described attempts to create video games for social change:

> The central conceit of the Internet: that you can change the world without having to actually do anything. Want to change America? Download the [President] Obama app. Want to fight the Iranian mullahs? Turn your Twitter icon green. Want to bring human rights to oppressed peoples? Play a video game about it. Because what matters isn't fighting autocrats or feeding the hungry or improving the conditions of Haitian farmers. What matters is knowing that you care about such things.

His point is that the Internet itself is "all about you."

Hopefully, that tide is changing. We're witnessing a wave of business leaders who are truly making a difference. Blake Mycoskie founded TOMS Shoes in 2006 with the purpose of giving away a pair of shoes to a child in need with every purchase. Father-and-son team Philip and Jordan Wagner founded Generosity Water and, in their first two years of operation, funded 108 water wells in sixteen countries serving more than fifty thousand people with clean, safe drinking water.

Clearly these visionary leaders are resonating with millions of people across America. It's time to realize that without moral courage and purpose, we'll never live lives of significance, and we'll never make a real difference.

Set priorities for your goals. A major part of successful living lies in the ability to put first things first. Indeed, the reason most major goals are not achieved is that we spend our time doing second things first.
—ROBERT J. MCKAIN, MOTIVATIONAL SPEAKER AND WRITER

The issue of moral courage is critical. It's the foundation for creating priorities. Simply put, priorities are what is important. But how do we know what our priorities should be?

We start by deciding what is important to us.

I'll never forget when one of my wife's best friends had a baby. She was a dedicated career woman who decided after a few nervous months at home that she would hire a nanny so she could go back to work and resume her career. Everything seemed fine for a while, until one day she came home from work to hear the excited nanny cry out in joy, "Guess what? Today the baby walked for the first time! You should have seen it!"

At that moment, the mom froze in horror. For the first time since her baby's birth, she realized that by going back to work, all the "firsts" in her child's life would be experienced by someone else. That jolt was like an explosion. She dropped her briefcase, called her boss, immediately resigned from her job, and never looked back.

At that moment she understood her priorities. She thought her career was number one in her life, but that day she realized her real priority was her family.

Certainly not everyone can afford to stay at home with his or her children, and each situation is different. But the point is, once you realize your priorities, everything naturally finds its proper position of importance in your life.

Strong lives are motivated by dynamic purposes.
—KENNETH HILDEBRAND, WRITER

Take out a sheet of paper and write down all the things that are important to you. Perhaps it's family life, personal integrity, your relationship with God, a new boyfriend or girlfriend, your reputation, or your career. Perhaps it's being a caregiver to a loved one in need, personal health, staying in shape, or personal relationships.

Don't get your priorities confused with your goals. Goals are what you want to accomplish. Priorities are what is important on the way to achieving those goals. For your life to change and your goals to matter, your goals must exist within your priorities.

For instance, if your goal is a career that requires a great deal of travel but your family life is a high priority, then the two might not be a good mix. If your goal is to be financially successful but your priorities are to spend most of your time hanging out with friends, then you need to reconsider one or the other. Or if a personal priority is honesty/integrity but your boss is trying to influence you to lie on a report or to "adjust" some numbers on the accounting statement, then you're going to have a problem.

What are your priorities? Let me show you a list to get you started. I've divided the list into two categories—personal priorities and business priorities. There are many more than these, but the list will help you understand what we're talking about.

PERSONAL PRIORITIES:	BUSINESS PRIORITIES:
honesty	consideration of employees
integrity	responsibility
trust	leadership
creativity	innovation
independence	product quality
spiritual commitment	promptness
financial security	teamwork
physical health	ethics
raising children	attitude
having a strong marriage	speed
love	work accuracy
education	financial accountability
compassion	
generosity	
confidence	

There are plenty of others, and you'll no doubt have some that aren't on this list. I'm not as interested in your specific personal priorities as much as that you realize that the sooner you *understand* your priorities, the sooner you'll be able to move forward with real change.

Now that you have your priority list, use that list to filter all the changes in your life. Every job, every project, and every task you want to accomplish should fit within the framework of your priorities. Think of it as the boundary of integrity that surrounds your life.

Why? Because it keeps you focused on your goal and eliminates the time wasters in your life.

MANAGING YOUR PRIORITIES MEANS MANAGING YOUR TIME

At the highest levels of American business, time is valued more highly than money. That's why CEOs of major corporations have private jets standing by at the airport. With a private jet, they can leave at the last minute, bypass all the airport security checks and ticket counters, arrive at a meeting one thousand miles away, and be back home in their own beds that night, ready to be in the office first thing in the morning. If they took a commercial flight, they would have to leave the office much earlier, endure all the hardships of modern-day travel, possibly miss the last flight back, spend the night in a local hotel, and then miss half the next day flying back home.

It's all about time. The more time an executive can spend leading his or her company instead of sitting on an airplane, the more valuable he or she is and the more profit the company can make.

The Bondage of E-mail

Remember when we used to actually be productive? Now most employees spend their day managing e-mails. In fact, recent studies indicate that 40 percent of a typical employee's day is spent sending or receiving e-mail. I like writer Julie Morgenstern's advice: never check your e-mail in the morning. Julie discovered the incredible time-suck of e-mail and learned that when you check e-mail first thing in the morning, the next thing you realize is that it's lunchtime and you're still managing e-mail messages. She realized it's much better to focus first on the top priority of the day. You'll see your productivity shoot up.

The technology that was supposed to free us up has simply created handcuffs, especially when it comes to smartphones, iPads, and other handheld devices. I recently met three very successful business leaders for dinner in San Diego. Great restaurant, fabulous meal, engaging conversation—except for one thing. One of the guests simply could not put down his BlackBerry. In spite of the atmosphere, excellent dinner companions, and fascinating discussion, he was chained to the device and could only put it down long enough to occasionally take a bite of his steak.

I wanted to smash it on the floor and ask what potential message could be so important that he was willing to sacrifice being in the moment with face-to-face friends?

Short Moments Matter

A few years ago, I started focusing my time on quick but positive goals. For instance, before, if I had fifteen minutes with nothing to do, I would assume it wasn't enough time to accomplish anything, so I would just chat with someone or get a soft drink from the kitchen. But once I began managing my time, I was amazed to learn just how much can be done in fifteen minutes. I could clean my desk, organize my files, edit a magazine article, make a phone call, back up my computer, jot down some creative new ideas, and more. With just little snippets of time, I now can harvest enormous productivity.

All because I made time a priority.

Things which matter most must never be
at the mercy of things which matter least.
—GOETHE

Priorities do not come second nature without our thinking about them. We have to constantly remind ourselves of priorities and keep them in the forefront of our minds. It's not about losing our way—after all, most of us won't suddenly wake up and lose our integrity, honesty, or desire for independence. In the rush and noise of modern living, however, it's easy to let our priorities get pushed into the background of our lives. Even though I've experienced a rush of productivity and accomplishment after learning to manage my time, I still have a tendency to watch too much TV, hang out with the guys, and waste time at the computer. Good time management is a daily discipline, just like working out at the gym.

One important aspect of not managing your priorities well is that you don't lose them all at once. Priorities are traded off a piece at a time. In the case of time management, you don't suddenly become a slob. More likely, you show up late for an appointment or miss a meeting. Then you waste a little time in the afternoons and start to enjoy it. Little by little, the priority gets shoved farther and farther back into the pile.

Therefore everyone who hears these words of mine and puts them into practice is like a wise man who built his house on the rock. The rain came down, the streams rose, and the winds blew and beat against that house; yet it did not fall, because it had its foundation on the rock. But everyone who hears these words of mine and does not put them into practice is like a foolish man who built his house on sand. The rain came down, the streams rose, and the winds blew and beat against that house, and it fell with a great crash. (Matthew 7:24–27 NIV)

Jesus taught about the importance of a solid foundation for your life. In the same way, priorities are the ground you build your future on because they anchor the rest of your life. With your priorities in order, you can build any type of structure because integrity, honesty, physical health, good time management, and other positive priorities can withstand any change or challenge you face.

Don't spend your life looking over your shoulder in fear because you lied on that report, cheated on your spouse, or transposed the final budget numbers to make the company look better. Don't join the office gossip that could damage an employee's future because it might help you move ahead. And don't trade your reputation for stock options, a bonus, or a promotion.

Your priorities are your foundation. Make sure they are the kind that last, and make sure they reflect your values, your aspirations, and your life.

Too many people spend too many years working in jobs that don't really reflect their personal priorities. As a result, every day their jobs are like sandpaper, rubbing against their spirits until they're raw and painful. It's like playing for the wrong team or helping the enemy.

The money may be great, your office window might have a gorgeous view, and your business card may have a fantastic title. But if you have to compromise your priorities, the price is too high. Priorities are something to value, develop, and cherish. Without them, you're drifting without a compass, a map, or a guide.

We all have friends who have made poor choices. In most cases, they made those bad choices because they didn't have the right priorities. Would you rather live your life with the pain of tough choices now or the pain of regret later?

BETTER CHOICES

The Keys to Strong Decision Making

It is our choices . . . that show what we truly are,
far more than our abilities.
—J. K. ROWLING, *HARRY POTTER AND THE CHAMBER OF SECRETS*

When you have to make a choice and don't make it,
that in itself is a choice.
—WILLIAM JAMES, NOVELIST

Everything that happens in our lives happens because of a choice. Do I get out of bed this morning? Do I go to work? Do I feed my family? Do I acquire the new company? Do I clean the house? Do I prepare for that big report? Do I read that new book on changing my life? Every day is an endless chain of decisions.

I'm a television producer and director, and from the moment I step onto the studio set, I'm faced with an unrelenting string of questions. Lighting, makeup, acting, staging, design, film, on and on. Actors asking about their performances, lighting options for the scene. What do we shoot first? What's the camera angle? The job of directing a television program or movie is an endless job of making choices.

Today, instead of choices and decisions, we live in a world where people are desperately looking for excuses. The "blame someone else" mentality has seeped into the very fabric of our culture to the point where frivolous lawsuits clog our courts and waste hundreds of millions of dollars each year.

When we make a mistake, we want it to be anyone's fault but our own. We refuse to take responsibility for our decisions, and as a result, we've created a culture of blame. We spill coffee in our lap, and it's the restaurant's fault because the coffee's too hot. We murder our neighbor, and it's because of our conflicted childhoods. We have sexual affairs because we're under too much stress. We cheat on tests at school because everyone else is doing it. The list continues.

Embracing change means taking responsibility for our own decisions.

I believe that we are solely responsible for our choices,
and we have to accept the consequences of every deed,
word, and thought throughout our lifetime.
—ELISABETH KÜBLER-ROSS, PSYCHIATRIST

You are at the point you are in life today because of a string of decisions you made yesterday. I call it the "waterfall effect" because every choice we make in life has consequences "downstream." In his book *Awaken the Giant Within*, Anthony Robbins put it this way:

As you look back over the last ten years, were there times when a different decision would have made your life radically different from today, either for better or for worse? Maybe, for example, you made a career decision that changed your life. Or maybe you failed to make one. Maybe you decided during the last ten years to get married—or divorced. You might have purchased a tape, a book, or attended a seminar and, as a result, changed your beliefs and actions. Maybe you decided to start exercising, or to give it up. It could be that you decided to stop smoking. Maybe you decided to move to another part of the country, or to take a trip around the world. How have these decisions brought you to this point in your life? (33).

It's not our environments, the people around us, or the conditions of our lives that determine our futures; it's the personal choices we make or don't make. Certainly, people who have grown up in abusive families, been surrounded by negative people, or been the victims of crime, extreme poverty, or physical handicaps have challenges most of us know little about and can hardly understand. But even within the context of a horrible upbringing, physical handicap, or negative situation, it's the choices we make in the context of those situations that make the real difference in our lives.

Actor Christopher Reeve could have easily given up after his freak horseback riding accident left him a quadriplegic, tethered to a breathing machine. Everyone would have understood if, after a successful life as a movie star, he had shrunk back and faced the rest of his life in resignation and defeat.

But Christopher Reeve chose a different path. He chose to be a fighter, an activist, and a role model to millions of people with and without physical limitations. He made a choice. In spite of his conditions, circumstances, and limitations, he made a positive decision to move forward.

Your ability to change your life is directly connected to your ability to make choices and to take responsibility for those choices.

» YOUR DAILY DECISIONS DETERMINE YOUR DESTINY.

Working in Hollywood, I've met lots of people who want to produce movies. At parties or social gatherings, they're quick to talk about their movie idea and how they're going to write an award-winning screenplay. They have the greatest goals and aspirations but never seem to actually get anything down on paper.

They have the *desire* to do it, but they have never made the *decision* to do it. Decision is always the by-product of commitment. When you commit to reaching a goal, you make a decision—a choice—and things start happening.

Good plans shape good decisions.
That's why good planning helps to make elusive dreams come true.
—LESTER R. BITTEL, WRITER

The desire to make good choices is one thing; actually *making* those choices when the time comes is quite another. It's one thing to decide you're going to stop drinking, but it's another thing to make that choice at the next party when the hostess hands you a martini. It's one thing to decide to deal with pornography, but another thing to make the right choice when you're in the office alone and realize how easy it is to find it on the Internet. It's easy to think about one day going back to college but never quite get around to signing up for a class.

Intentions and actions. Two different things.

We're not retreating, we're just advancing in another direction.
—GENERAL GEORGE S. PATTON

Every great leader has wrestled with difficult decisions. The cornerstone of great leadership is the ability to see information and then make the correct decision—even if that information is incomplete or inaccurate. In the business world, top executives aren't paid millions of dollars to carry briefcases, analyze data, or run meetings. They're paid to make decisions. At the highest corporate levels, billions of dollars hang in the balance, and correct decisions are critical.

Making those types of choices sometimes takes great courage. In *Fast Company* magazine, Senator John McCain wrote:

Without courage, all virtue is fragile: admired, sought after, professed, but held cheaply and surrendered without a fight. Winston Churchill called courage "the first of human qualities . . . *because it guarantees all the others." That's what we mean by the courage of our convictions . . .*

Love makes courage necessary. And it's love that makes courage possible for all of us to possess. You get courage by loving something more than your own well-being. When you love virtue, when you love freedom, when you love other people, you find the strength to demand courage of yourself and those who aspire to lead you. Only then will you find the courage, as Eleanor Roosevelt put it, "to do the thing you think you cannot do." (emphasis added)

Writer E. M. Forster said, "Either life entails courage, or it ceases to be life." The kind of courage you display doesn't have to happen on the battlefield or in a corporate boardroom. Courage happens when a mom speaks up at a PTA meeting, a worker defends a fellow employee wrongly criticized at the office, or a person makes the decision to confront a friend about suspected drug abuse.

Courage is what takes you from intention to action and from debate to decision.

Begin today. Every time you procrastinate making a choice, you take a detour on the road of change. Success is simply the result of a lifetime of choices, and every day you delay puts your future success on hold.

Here are the secrets I've discovered for making better choices in life:

1. FIND THE BEST INFORMATION AVAILABLE.

Great decision makers are great learners. They know that making decisions is about balancing information and that often the person with the best information wins. What changes do you want to make in your life? Whatever the change, get the right information first.

Want to stop drinking? Find as much information as you can about treatment programs. Find the right program for you, and make a good decision.

Want to advance in your career? Read books, listen to podcasts or audiobooks, scour trade magazines, go to the right seminars and conferences. Learn everything you can about the next level in your career so that you can make the best decisions possible.

Need to go back to school? There are lots of colleges out there, and amazing numbers of people fail because they simply can't make a decision on which college to attend. Check schools out on the Internet, order catalogs and brochures, visit a few in person. Get the right information to be sure it's the best choice and offers what you need, at the right location, and fits your budget.

No intelligent decision can be made without the right information, so to make the right choices, do your homework first.

One's philosophy is not best expressed in words; it is
expressed in the choices one makes . . . and the choices
we make are ultimately our responsibility.
—ELEANOR ROOSEVELT

2. FIND GOOD DECISION MAKERS AND LEARN FROM THEM.

Who are the people you know who make the best choices? They don't have to be high-level business leaders. One might be a soccer mom who understands the power of good decisions. Perhaps it's your pastor or a friend in the community. You are surrounded by people who make choices every day. Find the ones who make strong choices and spend time with them—especially those who wrestle with the same types of challenges you face.

Early in my life, I learned the power of associating with successful people. I heard a story about a successful businessman who was frustrated that he was only making five hundred thousand dollars a year. By most standards, he was rich, but he wanted to move to the next salary level. At a business conference, he met a highly motivated real estate agent who was making more than one million dollars a year and asked the agent his secret. The real estate agent replied, "It's about association. I decided I wanted access to million-dollar ideas, so I associate with million-dollar people."

That real estate agent was right. Whatever your salary or career level, if you want to get to the next step, stop spending so much time with people at your level and begin to stretch. Find people at the level you want to reach and begin associating with them. Is this snobbish? Absolutely not. There's nothing snobbish about feeding a champion athlete expensive food because coaches know that what goes into an athlete dictates how well he or she will perform. If you want to perform better in your family, in your company, in your relationships, or in your personal life, start feeding yourself from the riches of successful people.

> I believe it would be a safe assumption that the great majority of people work at jobs in which they find very little personal satisfaction. Without proper training on how to make wise choices in one's life, the chances are very slim anyone will make them.
> —SIDNEY MADWED, MOTIVATIONAL WRITER

3. MAKE GOOD DECISIONS EVERY DAY.

Start a habit of making strong decisions. Don't begin ordering people around and become a jerk, but stop putting things off or avoiding. Start making good decisions today. You don't have to start out making world-changing decisions about the war on terrorism or world hunger; just start with small things—that pile of papers on your desk, for instance. Just as an athlete trains his muscles for a sporting event, your decision-making muscles need to be trained, and the key is starting slow. When you see what can be accomplished in your life—even by small choices—you'll experience what I call a "decision rush" that will give you the excitement and energy to move to the next level.

Look around. What are the choices you've avoided in your life and the decisions you've been putting off? Nothing is too small or silly to begin with, because the small decisions start training you for the big ones.

Honor isn't about making the right choices.
It's about dealing with the consequences.
—MIDORI KOTO, *HIGHLANDER* CHARACTER

4. MAKE TOUGH DECISIONS ON A REGULAR BASIS.

As you grow in your decision-making skills, don't avoid the big ones. Learn to face one difficult dilemma each day and make a decision on it. Making tough decisions is all about perspective. My daughters, Kelsey and Bailey, wrestle with choices that I wouldn't think twice about because I've had far more experience. Work the decision-making muscle and expand your ability to handle the hardest decisions in life.

5. BEGIN TO GROW IN THE CHOICES YOU MAKE.

Making right choices comes from experience. Every time you make a choice—either wrong or right—learn from it. Start building a "decision data bank" that will help you the next time you're faced with a challenge and need to make a choice. Every choice has a consequence, and we have to learn to live within those decisions. Many people refuse to make choices because of the potential consequences, but thank God for people who have the courage to see beyond potential failure and make the hard choices in life.

Once decision making becomes a habit, you'll begin to enjoy the freedom, accomplishment, and joy it will release in your life. Too many people sit around waiting for other people to make choices for them.

» **REAL FREEDOM LIES IN MAKING YOUR OWN DECISIONS, PLANNING YOUR OWN CHOICES, DEALING WITH THE CONSEQUENCES, AND DETERMINING YOUR OWN DESTINY.**

Like the rest of this journey of change, making right choices isn't always easy. If you've lived a life of bad decisions, you'll be carrying a lot of baggage that may be tough to lose. It might even shock you to discover that you'll probably have friends who won't like this new person who's taking charge of his or her own life and making positive decisions. Many of your friends and family members will prefer to keep hanging out, blaming society, the government, or their parents for their problems. They won't like someone who suddenly causes them to confront the real problems that are holding them back.

My advice is to be sensitive and gracious to their frustrations, but don't give in. Not for a moment. In fact, let this statement be your first choice:

I'll never go back to blaming others, waiting for others to make my decisions, or giving up my freedom of choice. Starting today, I realize it's not the conditions or circumstances of my life that are holding me back, it's the choices I make or don't make. From now on, I'm getting the right information, spending time with good decision makers, making tough choices every day, and growing in those choices. I will never look back, and I choose to move forward into the future that awaits me.

I can tell you, from living in earthquake country, the most powerful jolts are the ones that happen in contained spaces. Earthquakes have a lot more impact inside a building than in an open field. That's why our next jolt is about boundaries and how drawing lines can increase the intensity and power of your life.

BORDERS

The Map of Who You Are

Boundaries define us. They define what is me and what is not me.
A boundary shows me where I end and someone else begins,
leading me to a sense of ownership.
—DR. HENRY CLOUD AND DR. JOHN TOWNSEND, *BOUNDARIES*

In the age of social media, personal boundaries have become blurred to the point of being erased. People live their lives online and don't think twice about sharing the most personal, intimate information with the world.

As a new generation enters the workforce, they're discovering that living online has its downside. Those pictures of getting drunk during spring break at Daytona Beach seemed cute when posted on their Facebook or MySpace pages. But now, as they start job interviews, they discover the first thing employers do is an online search. Suddenly, pictures of puking on the lawn half-naked don't seem so cute anymore.

While that may seem a comical example, many experts believe the age of privacy is over. I sat on a plane recently with a government analyst whose job is to profile potential terrorists for our military leadership. He explained the irony of privacy advocates getting upset over the Patriot Act, created after 9/11. He said not to worry about the Patriot Act. The *existing* databases are staggering, and if people knew how much personal information is already out there, they would be astonished.

The owner of a data mining company I talked with agreed. His company researches information on consumers for the advertising and marketing industry, and he confirmed that in a connected, online world, there is no privacy anymore. There's even an iPhone app that does online background searches of personal databases—including the criminal activity of anyone you type into the program. Anyone can find out just about anything on anybody.

How do we come to terms with a world where the price of convenience is giving up our privacy?

> » **WE CAN START TO TAKE OUR LIVES BACK**
> **WITH THE ABILITY TO SAY NO.**

Where should we create boundaries? Where do we draw the line in saying yes and no? When do others push us too far? How do we know when others are taking advantage of us?

Two issues are at stake here:

1. How much do we reveal about ourselves publicly?
2. Whenever we begin to change, people will notice, and not everyone will be happy with it.

I worked with a television soundman who came from a relatively poor background with little education or training. He had married young, and his wife was in the same situation—no real education, no ambition, and no clear future. Because they were both so much alike, they lived happily together for many years, until my friend attended a business conference that changed his life.

For the first time he realized the potential in the television industry and his own personal possibilities for growth. He went home with a real commitment to change his life. He first decided to enroll in night school so he could get his credentials as an audio engineer. Then he began attending more conferences, spending time with experienced engineers, and expanding his knowledge of the business. It didn't take long for his supervisors to notice. Before long he received a significant raise, was promoted to assistant engineer at the facility, and got a bigger office and more responsibility. He was thrilled. All the hard work, extra effort, and changes he was making were paying off.

His life was fantastic—except for one area.

His marriage.

While my friend had spent the last year learning and growing, his wife had stayed exactly where she'd always been. She wasn't interested in change. She liked life just the way it was and wasn't the least bit interested in this new life her husband was enjoying. That's when they began growing apart. First, they had less and less to talk about over dinner because the new things my friend was interested in didn't interest his wife. When he wanted to travel to workshops and seminars, his wife never wanted to go because she preferred to stay at home. Slowly, their lives began moving in two different directions.

As he grew in the industry, he began taking more care in how he dressed, but she preferred the "old husband," who wore jeans and T-shirts. She began criticizing him for pursuing new interests, new friends, and his new career.

Then she played the guilt card: "You don't care about our family anymore. It's all about you these days. What happened to the way we used to be?" And the manipulation began to work. He loved her and wanted to stay married, but she gave him no options: "If you want to stay with me, then you've got to stop this nonsense with your career and spend more time with me."

To make a long story short, her plan worked. Little by little, he stopped learning, meeting new people, and taking on new responsibilities at work. As she manipulated him, he became more withdrawn on the job and stayed mostly in his office. He hung his new suits in the closet and began wearing his old clothes again. His supervisors noticed a change, but he refused to talk about it, and before long, he was his former self once again.

The bright future, unlimited possibilities, and destiny that lay within his grasp had now become an illusion.

Keeping a marriage intact is one of the greatest accomplishments anyone can pursue, but because my friend didn't understand boundaries, he allowed his wife to manipulate and coerce him into becoming someone else. Because he refused to say no and clearly understand his boundaries, he allowed someone else to control and determine his future.

As you make changes in your life, you will encounter many people like my friend's wife. People who prefer their drinking buddy, people who like having someone to gossip with, or who want to keep things the way they've always been.

Even at the highest levels of business, control and manipulation are commonplace. Boards can manipulate CEOs, senior executives can manipulate staff members, and managers can manipulate employees.

That's why you need to understand personal boundaries. We all have friends who tend to be domineering, overpowering, and sometimes obnoxious. It comes from a number of reasons—insecurity, powerlessness, a need to feel as if they're in charge. Whatever the reason, you have to move ahead.

There are some cases where serious psychological and even pathological issues are involved. This sometimes happens in the case of abuse victims, whose lives are manipulated by the abuser to keep them isolated and away from other people. In other cases, I've encountered unhealthy relationships between mothers and sons, where mothers tend to influence their sons to an amazing extent far into adulthood, as if their sons have some type of weird spell cast over them. Those are serious problems that require serious help. If someone is violating your boundaries to that extent or you're experiencing intense manipulation, I would urge you to seek professional advice and counseling.

Most people, on the other hand, just wrestle with people who refuse to honor their decisions and their individuality.

Early in my career, I briefly worked for a television producer who liked to dominate and control his employees. He would carry a gun in his briefcase to intimidate people and would humiliate and embarrass them in front of others at the studio.

I've seen others who used money and salaries to control workers, or used office perks to favor some and hurt others. Even in an age of political correctness, sexual manipulation still happens at the office.

Realize that having strong boundaries helps other people understand who we are.

When we learn to say no, we're helping other people learn where to draw the line in dealing with us. How far they can go with jokes, social matters, romantic notions, appropriate behavior, and more. Although we're often afraid we'll hurt people's feelings by drawing solid lines, we're actually doing them a favor and saving them from embarrassment. It may be awkward and uncomfortable, but it's nothing compared to the potential pain of having to confront them later. Just speak up. Let people know where your boundaries are and how to respect them.

» BOUNDARIES ARE A CRITICAL KEY TO TAKING OWNERSHIP OF OUR LIVES.

More than five hundred years before Christ, Greek philosopher Thales said, "Know thyself," and his advice is just as important today. Knowing our strengths, weaknesses, gifts, talents, and abilities is an absolute in the journey of change.

Make it thy business to know thyself,
which is the most difficult lesson in the world.
—MIGUEL DE CERVANTES, NOVELIST

I'm amazed at the number of people who fail in life because they haven't examined their lives closely. They don't know what makes them motivated, depressed, angry, or tired. They don't know their limits or their stress points. It's similar to the red line on the speedometer of your car. We all have days and sometimes weeks when we're in overdrive. But people who know their boundaries recognize when they kick into the red line, and they adjust accordingly. They realize that within a short time, they must have a break or a vacation. But those who don't understand their boundaries and limitations live in overdrive 24/7. They live in a perpetual state of stress, working too hard at the office, juggling too many activities with the kids, or overcommitting their time and resources. And before long, they begin to break down.

Worse, they allow others to exert far too much control over their lives.

Understand your boundaries. Know your limitations.

Personal boundaries are invisible, and unless you point them out, you'll become invisible as well.

THE POWER OF FOCUS

Selective Thinking Is the Key to Breakthrough

A mind troubled by doubt cannot focus on the course to victory.
—ARTHUR GOLDEN, *MEMOIRS OF A GEISHA*

*Focus 90% of your time on solutions
and only 10% of your time on problems.*
—ANTHONY J. D'ANGELO, *THE COLLEGE BLUE BOOK*

We can't talk about disruption without mentioning the advertising industry. Right now, advertising and marketing are experiencing a very challenging time, and change is happening on a daily basis. I know because I'm a cofounder of a production company that produced two Super Bowl commercials in 2008. At the time, broadcasting thirty-second spots during the Super Bowl cost $2.2 million each. That doesn't even count the cost of *producing* the commercials, which can be in the $1 million-plus range for high-profile spots.

Why in the world do Super Bowl spots cost so much? *The power of focus.* When millions of people are focused with such intensity, thirty seconds is all you need to get your message across.

Major advertisers have long understood the power of focus. As a media consultant, I meet people all the time who tell me, "Television doesn't affect me. I can watch for hours and it doesn't have any impact at all." I read recently that the average American watches more than four hours of television a night, and my experience indicates that it's not so unusual for people (especially young people) to view up to seven hours of television and computer enter-tainment on a daily basis!

People may think it doesn't have any impact, but most professionals like me beg to differ. Advertising agencies know that thirty-second commercials affect behavior, and they are willing to spend millions of dollars based on that belief. And if thirty seconds affects behavior, think of the impact four to seven hours a day can have.

The point? In television as in life, focus matters.

In the last ten years, "multitasking" has become all the rage. Doing multiple tasks at the same time has become the ultimate symbol of accomplishment. If you can write a book, make phone calls, keep your appointments, finalize the presentation, and solve an employee problem all at the same time, you're con-sidered a corporate genius in today's economy.

I know, because I've become a master at multitasking. I'm sure it's con-nected to the fact that I've always been easily distracted, but believe me, I can juggle a lot and survive. Focusing was always a little difficult for me, so I made up for it by doing a ton of different things all at once. I could answer e-mail, make phone calls, finish a TV script, and organize my desk at the same time without even thinking about it. In fact, I could juggle at that pace for hours without a second thought.

But then I noticed some interesting research that indicated multitasking wasn't as productive as it seemed. In fact, balancing multiple tasks and jug-gling projects was far less successful than I thought. I learned that when people like me multitask, we make many more mistakes and often end up taking even longer to correct those mistakes.

That's when I started researching the power of focus—doing one task at a time and doing it really well. In a digital age, it doesn't seem quite as fashion-able, but the more I study it, the more I learn the benefits of this little-used skill.

> » FOCUS ALLOWS YOU TO TAKE CONTROL OF ALL YOUR SKILLS, INTELLIGENCE, AND RESOURCES AND PUT THEM TO WORK ON YOUR IMMEDIATE PROBLEM.

Instead of doing five tasks relatively well, or with average skill, focus allows you to turn all that energy and effort into doing one thing at the peak of your abilities. And the results can be absolutely amazing.

This very book was delayed because of my initial lack of focus. I've had this information inside me for years, but I continued to allow distractions to take me off course. Running two companies, consulting with numerous organizations, directing commercials and television programs—all pulled my attention away from the real dream of helping people through the power of change. As a result, for the longest time I would only work on the book in small snippets of time stolen away from other tasks and projects. I would either wake up early in the morning to write for a few hours, or grab a few minutes before bed. I actually wrote the last chapter on an airline flight between Atlanta and Los Angeles. As a result, I was writing as many as four different chapters at the same time. A few paragraphs here, a few there, and then I would shift to another section of the book when something else came to mind.

In this culture, where multitasking is prized above all things, I should have probably won some award for juggling my normal routine and then finding fragments of time to write a book. But I finally realized that it wasn't just my schedule that was becoming fragmented; the book was fragmented as well. As I read my rough drafts, I discovered that any sense of overall direction, theme, or sense of completeness was lacking. The book had snippets of good information but was lacking any real depth and wholeness.

So I decided to focus. I redesigned my schedule so that I could focus the time, energy, and effort on completing the book. I threw out the incomplete sections and started devoting more time (undistracted time) to the writing process. I shut the door, refused to answer the phone during certain parts of the day, and started to focus on writing.

When that happened, I noticed something amazing. The focus allowed me to go deep.

SLEEP RESEARCH AND THE POWER OF FOCUS

It was much like what researchers have discovered about REM sleep. In our sleep patterns we desperately need time in our REM sleep. It's where we dream and how we recover from the day. Scientists have discovered that skipping this most productive stage of sleep has devastating results.

Researchers have conflicting ideas about why we dream during REM sleep, but one of the theories is particularly compelling to me. Some scientists believe that dreaming allows our subconscious minds to "sort through" the experiences, thoughts, and ideas that have been floating around and helps us "connect the dots" or put them all into perspective. That would explain why our dreams mix and match various experiences—even though they make no sense on the surface. Perhaps our subconscious is trying to sort things out— putting experiences into a perspective that we would never consider with our conscious minds. The result has fascinated us since the beginning of time and spawned all kinds of dream interpretation theories, occult practices, mediums, and wacko ideas.

» SLEEP ON IT.

This research has also given credence to the old phrase "Sleep on it." My mother (and most likely yours as well) always told me to "sleep on it" when I was wrestling with a problem, challenge, or dilemma for which I just couldn't find the answer.

Guess what? Mom may just have been right. (Just as with a million other things.)

Researchers today believe that when we have a difficult problem for which we need an answer, if we'll think on the problem right before bedtime, our subconscious minds can work it out. In *Newsweek* magazine's feature story, "What Dreams Are Made Of," writers Barbara Kantrowitz and Karen Springen, with Pat Wingert and Josh Ulick, report evidence that dreaming helps certain types of learning:

> Some researchers have found that dreaming about physical tasks, like a gymnast's floor routine, enhances performance. Dreaming can also help people find solutions to elusive problems. "Anything that is very visual may get extra help from dreams," says Deirdre Barrett, assistant professor at Harvard Medical School and editor of the journal *Dreaming*. In her book *The Committee of Sleep*, she describes how

artists like Jasper Johns and Salvador Dali found inspiration in their dreams. In her own research on problem solving through dreams, Barrett has found that even ordinary people can solve simple problems in their lives (like how to fit old furniture into a new apartment) if they focus on the dilemma before they fall asleep.

One way I use dreams is by keeping a notebook on the side of the bed. I'll often wake up in the middle of the night with ideas, stories, and illustrations that help whatever challenges I happen to be facing at the time. I've discovered that if I wait until morning, I'll forget the idea, because our thinking is very delicate during dream states. It's very hard to remember the first things that come to mind after waking—especially in the middle of the night. So keep a notebook by your bed and get into the habit of writing down what comes to mind as soon as you wake up.

» WHAT DISTRACTIONS ARE KEEPING YOU FROM ACHIEVING YOUR GOALS?

Is it a personal problem, like laziness, lack of ambition, the tug of pornography, the lure of the party life, or the well-meaning disturbance of good friends who want more of your time? Or what about business distractions, like spending too much time on the Internet, talking with coworkers, the wrong office environment, poor equipment, being hypercritical of the company, or a host of other issues?

I recently worked with one client who was hyperattentive to the minutest details. Taking normal care of fine points is important, but this executive took it to the extreme. Whenever we would turn in a report or a television program, he would take enormous time to view it and send us a list of every possible error, inconsistency, or problem. I'm talking way over the top here—crooked staples in the report, minor grammar issues, a bad frame of video (keep in mind that video has thirty frames per second), or the slightest audio deviation. We produce programs of the highest quality, but in thirty years of producing, I'd never experienced anything like this guy.

Then one day he came to me exhausted and overworked. He was complaining of all the responsibilities of his job and how he desperately needed help. I shared with him the idea that he might be allowing his manic attention to details to become a distraction. Anyone spending that much time looking for microscopic problems would wear himself out. Apparently, in his extreme effort to look good to the president, he was killing himself trying to find anything that might get him noticed. But his enormous effort to find tiny issues no one else would ever see was keeping him from focusing on the most significant parts of his job.

We'll discuss distractions in more detail in a later chapter, but for now, whatever your distractions may be, begin today to fill the void with something you can positively focus on. Identify your areas of distraction and start relentlessly practicing focus.

» TAKE THE INITIATIVE TO CHANGE YOUR SITUATION.

Too many people complain and expect someone else to solve their problems. Perhaps your desk isn't right, you have a slow computer, or your office is too cramped, and you're waiting for the company to make the change.

You may not be able to afford making major changes yourself, but I would urge you to consider the steps you can take right now. Perhaps you can't afford a faster computer, but you could offer to split the cost with the company. After all, if your computer is keeping you from doing excellent work, being noticed, and getting a promotion, then what are you accomplishing by waiting? Learn to take control of your story because if you don't, someone else will.

Is your office arranged in the most productive way? Is your desk located in a place where every person who walks by your door is a distraction? Are you too open for interruptions? If you have an assistant, is he or she helping you maximize your focus?

Another key to learning focus is what I call the *field of vision*. Your field of vision is the immediate issues you face during the day—literally, what you are seeing. One of the keys to maintaining focus is to keep the things you're focusing on in your field of vision at all times. I've discovered that most people are visual learners. We live in a culture that has moved from a text-based culture to a visually based culture.

Whatever you want to focus on, keep it directly in front of you in the form of pictures, objects, or files. Keep it in your field of vision.

I have two sets of files in my office. My assistant keeps the master file in the cabinets outside her office, but I keep files for immediate projects on my desk. I can see them, think about them, and if I'm not doing something about them, those files act as a constant reminder. Our production supervisor keeps an updated list of our projects, my assistant keeps my to-do list, and they both make a practice of making sure I see those lists on a regular basis. By keeping those projects in my field of vision, it helps me eliminate anything else that may be competing for my time.

Make a list of the top five things that you feel you need to focus on right now. Once you get those projects, priorities, or issues on the list, begin to eliminate any distractions that would keep you from intense, focused concentration on accomplishing those changes in your life. Finally, keep those items in your field of vision. Keep the list on your desk, or better yet, keep physical reminders in front of you. If it's a book you need to read, keep it in your bag; if it's a project, keep the folder on your desk. Begin today practicing the power of focus and let it begin to clarify the changes and goals that will keep you on the journey toward change.

A CHANGE OF HABIT

Breaking Destructive Patterns of Behavior

The second half of a man's life is made up of nothing but the habits he has acquired during the first half.
—FYODOR DOSTOEVSKY, RUSSIAN NOVELIST

A dictionary defines *habit* as "a recurrent, often unconscious pattern of behavior that is acquired through frequent repetition." But there's also a negative definition for the word *habit*: "an addiction—especially to a narcotic drug."

Habit is a powerful thing—much like the overwhelming pull of a drug, as noted in the second definition. Breaking habits is one of the most difficult things a man or woman can do. You would probably admit that many of your habits are negative, but the fact is, when you learn to break those negative habits and begin to harness positive behaviors, your life will change exponentially—because habits are repeated. And anything done over and over again will soon become part of your personality.

» BUT WHAT IF WE COULD CREATE POSITIVE HABITS?

It's been said that the only thing constant is change. But let me take that a bit further and say that when change becomes constant—or habitual—your life begins evolving to a new level.

Most experts would say that consistency is the key to everything. I dated a girl in college who wanted to be a concert pianist. Her life was designed around practicing the piano for at least four hours per day. It definitely cut back on our dating life, but I saw how regular, constant practice transformed her into a brilliant pianist. A professional athlete has to practice on a consistent basis if he or she is to become a champion.

What do you want to be? A better leader, a champion athlete, a successful entrepreneur, a real estate mogul, a movie producer?

How often do you practice?

Perhaps you can't actually make a movie, sell real estate, or lead an army every day, but you can practice the skills that successful people in your industry have acquired. Make it a habit so you'll do it without thinking, because that's when things start happening.

And while we're talking about practice, let me explode the common myth that practice makes perfect. As legendary football coach Vince Lombardi said, "Practice does not make perfect. Only *perfect* practice makes perfect." My college girlfriend would not have benefited one bit from all those long hours of practice if she hadn't been practicing correctly. We have to take the time to learn the right techniques, get the right advice and coaching, and make sure every time we practice, we're doing it correctly. Good habits come out of good practice.

Search the Internet or your local bookstore and you'll find plenty of resources for changing habits. Smoking, overeating, laziness, lack of motivation, overspending, lack of exercise—there are plenty of reasons to break negative habits and plenty of organizations, self-help groups, books, and teaching videos that testify to America's dark descent into too much smoking, eating, drinking, spending, and a host of other ills that plague our society.

Some people have extremely negative habits, and in a few cases they can contribute to injury, illness, or death. In those cases, I urge you to seek professional help from a doctor, mental health counselor, or pastor. Too many people look for easy answers to difficult challenges. The techniques in this book can get you moving in new directions and transform your thinking about change. But if you're facing serious obesity, addiction to drugs, gambling, sex, or similar life-destroying situations, I strongly suggest that along with this book, you seek professional help from qualified health care or counseling professionals.

But in most cases, a regular program of repetition and accountability can start you on the path to releasing your destructive habits, and opening the door to new, positive habits can impact your life in exciting ways. Some experts suggest a ten-day program, and others suggest up to thirty days or more, depending on the issue. To be honest, I've never seen compelling research that supports a particular number of days. Everyone is different, and everyone's "habit sensitivity" is set at different levels. Personally, I recommend at least ten days to change significant habits in most people.

Regardless of how entrenched your habits are, how do you break them? What do you do in those ten days?

1. FIRST, ISOLATE THE HABITS YOU WANT TO BREAK.

They might be small habits, like drumming your fingers on a desk when you're nervous, or twitching your nose in a meeting. They might be small, but they may drive your coworkers, boss, or spouse crazy. Small to you may be huge to others.

My wife tells me I have a rather annoying habit of making circles around my mouth with my finger when I'm thinking. I don't notice it, and I imagine it helps me concentrate, but it drives her nuts. Sitting in a movie, in church, or in a meeting, she'll catch me in the act, grab my hand, and pull it away from my mouth. Very small thing to me, very big thing to her.

By the way—just because you have a small habit doesn't mean it won't be hard to break. Very often the small habits are the most difficult to change because they work "under the radar." We usually don't even notice them, so it's difficult to alter our behavior. That's a key reason for our first step—isolating the habit—because it makes us notice.

On the other hand, you might want to change a really significant habit. I don't have to take the time to remind you how some bad habits can whittle away at your career or relationships. Habits like these are career killers, marriage killers, and can permanently end a promising future.

"But Phil, you're being overly dramatic. Showing up late doesn't matter that much." To others, showing up late means you don't respect their time and if you don't respect their time, you won't respect them. It may not matter to you, but believe me, it matters to the person constantly having to wait for you.

"But my reports don't have to be perfect." The smallest mistakes in reports or other correspondence can cost plenty. A misplaced comma, period, or quotation has changed the meaning and result of major projects. A misquoted statement or story can result in legal action. A mistake with a single number can cost a company millions of dollars. Mistakes in business can have serious consequences.

> » **HABITS CAN HAVE ENORMOUS CONSEQUENCES—NOT JUST FOR US BUT FOR OUR LOVED ONES AS WELL.**

Isolate your habits. Make a conscious list so you'll begin to notice the things you want to change.

2. NEXT, MAKE A NOTE ABOUT THE HABIT.

Notice how often you perform the habit and make a note. Call attention to it. Make it a big deal. Part of the reason we let our habits grow is that we let them live in the invisible world. Just like circling my mouth with my finger when I'm thinking. I don't notice it, and because I don't notice it, I continue the habit.

Noting the habit means writing it down—making note—and calling attention. Negative habits are the enemy to a successful life, and any military commander will tell you the key to defeating an enemy is to make the enemy visible. Radar, sonar, infrared, and satellite tracking are technologies designed to make the invisible, visible. When we can see the enemy clearly, we have the best chance of defeating it.

When you notice a bad habit and call attention to it, it allows you to see how often it disrupts your life or how many times you do it. Perhaps for the first time, you'll see not only why it drives your friends and coworkers nuts but also how it negatively impacts your life as well.

3. AFTER YOU'VE MADE NOTE OF THE HABIT, TAKE THE TIME TO EVALUATE AND UNDERSTAND IT.

Think about the habit and how that behavior can be broken and eliminated. What will it take to change?

When I work with organizations on strategic thinking and planning, I use the question, "What will have to be aligned for this to happen?"

In other words, to accomplish our goal for the organization, what steps will have to be in place? What will have to be changed in order to reach our goal of $100 million in sales? What will have to be determined to design a more creative environment for our employees? What will have to be in process to meet our goals for next year?

» WHAT WILL HAVE TO BE ALIGNED IN YOUR LIFE TO DEFEAT YOUR NEGATIVE HABITS?

I met a man who was wrestling with pornography. He wasn't a hard-core addict, but he knew it was a problem for him and wanted to put a stop to it before it gained control of his life. At times he would sneak adult magazines into his office or rent an adult movie in his hotel room on a business trip or view Internet porn on his computer after work. I suggested that he shortcut opportunities to let his habit kick in and that he avoid even the temptation. We outlined areas that would help. We purchased a software program that not only blocks pornographic websites but also sends an e-mail to his wife if he tries to access an adult site. He began avoiding newsstands in airports because of the pervasive way they advertise and display provocative magazines. And he began asking for adult movies to be blocked as a normal part of the check-in process at hotels.

We blocked the opportunities for his habit to express itself. Purchasing the correct software, clear avoidance, proper accountability—all those things had to be in place for him to conquer his habit.

Recently I met Delatorro L. McNeal II, a professional speaker and success coach. "Del" is one of the most motivated people I've ever met, and we became acquainted when he was on the set of a television program we were shooting. Del told me that early in his life he found himself stuck in a terrible family situation and, as a result, he was labeled an "at-risk child" by the local school system. As an African-American young man, he was trapped in the inner city with limited options, and after a few years the "at-risk" label stuck. He began to view himself as at-risk and soon realized that label dictated his future.

But one day, he met a teacher who changed his life. She sat him down, looked him directly in the eye, and said, "Delatorro, you're not a child *at risk*, you're a child *at possibility*." In a single moment, she changed his label from one of *risk* to one of *possibility*, and in that moment she changed the way he viewed himself and his world.

Since that time Del has spent his life helping other people overcome their labels and see their future in a different light. It's all about conditioning. Today in his presentations to young people, he illustrates the power of conditioning with the results of a study done on fleas. When researchers put a group of fleas in a container with a lid, they immediately tried to jump out but then hit the lid. Even with the tiny intelligence of a flea, it didn't take long for them to realize that when they tried to jump out of the container, it hurt. Not long after, the researchers took off the lid, and guess what? The fleas did not jump out of the container, even though without a lid it would have been an easy leap to freedom.

The lesson hits young people like a rocket. Whatever you're conditioned to do, you'll do it whether the conditions continue or not. Label a child a loser or at risk, and he'll consider himself a loser or an at-risk child for the rest of his life. It's all about the power of habits and the labels those habits represent.

But jolt a child's thinking by calling him a champion and see what happens. If you had a tough childhood, think of how your life might have changed if your parents had encouraged you more, believed in you more, and considered you a champion in life.

And imagine what would have happened if those beliefs had become habits.

As I stood there listening to Del, I thought about the millions of young people around the country who are regularly told, "You're stupid" or "You'll never make it" or "You'll never amount to anything." Those labels are thoughtless, ignorant, damaging, and destructive.

> » **NEVER FORGET THE POWER OF LABELS—IN YOUR LIFE AND IN THE LIVES OF OTHERS.**

What will have to be aligned for your habits to change? Evaluate the negative habits you've written down and then write what you'll have to do to change those habits. In one man's case, it was simple things like computer software, avoiding certain situations, and accountability. In your case, it might be seeing a doctor, agreeing with your boss or spouse, or rearranging your priorities.

Give it ten days and see what happens.

Open yourself up to the world of your invisible habits and begin making the changes that can transform your life.

REVIEW
Jolt What Matters

Make the decision today to take control of your life.

1. What do I need to do to make stronger choices in my life?
2. I am the only person controlling my life and my decisions. In what areas and with whom do I need to commit to stronger boundaries?
3. In what areas do I need to practice better focus?
4. What negative baggage and issues do I need to release?
5. In what areas of my life do I need to commit to breaking destructive patterns?
6. Write a statement of commitment, using your answers to the above questions. For example: I commit to _____ in order to make stronger choices. I commit to establish stronger boundaries with _____. (Continue with questions 3–5.)

JOLT
YOUR
POTENTIAL

PERSONAL GROWTH IS NOT AN OPTION

Never Stop Learning

*There are no great limits to growth because there are
no limits of human intelligence, imagination, and wonder.*
—RONALD REAGAN, PRESIDENT OF THE UNITED STATES

*Create the kind of climate in your organization where
personal growth is expected, recognized, and rewarded.*
—AUTHOR UNKNOWN

Personal growth can be daunting in an age when technology changes on a daily basis. Just when you thought you understood your TV remote, a new one comes out that also controls the Internet, the lights, and the washing machine. As a result, millions of people have just given up on learning anything new—believing that they can't possibly keep up with the explosion of newfangled information.

Knowledge and intelligence are wonderful assets. Obviously, the more someone knows, the more potential he or she has for weighing the facts, understanding different perspectives, and making good decisions. But growth is more than just learning information. The truth is, universities are filled with brilliant people who are personal failures. Our greatest innovators and most creative people aren't always the smartest. In studying leadership over the years, I've discovered that the greatest leaders aren't always the most intelligent executives in the company. In Hollywood, the most brilliant artists and filmmakers are often miserable failures in their personal and family lives.

» KNOWLEDGE IS IMPORTANT,
BUT THE REAL ASSET IS GROWTH.

Growth is what we do with knowledge. Growth is where we take our knowledge, how we apply it, and how we use it in our everyday lives.

Leadership expert John Maxwell taught me long ago to change my orientation from *goals* to *growth*. When he said those words, it was a revelation. I'd always learned that goals were important, and I tried and tried to use a system of reaching goals, but I'd always struggled with it. I could see that goals motivated lots of people and helped focus their energy, but reaching goals always left me empty and unsatisfied.

But when John showed me how to focus my attention on *growth*, everything suddenly fell into place. The process taught me that goals are great, but when we reach a goal, we're finished. But with growth, it's a never-ending process—always learning, always moving forward, and always achieving.

I hope that when I reach the end of my life, there will be a couple of good books on my nightstand. I want to learn and grow until my last breath.

Leadership and learning are indispensable to each other.
—JOHN F. KENNEDY, PRESIDENT OF THE UNITED STATES

Since first hearing about the importance of growth, I've patterned my life around that concept. Ten years after graduating from college, I earned a master's degree, and twenty-six years after college, I earned a PhD. A few years ago, I switched from a PC to a Mac, and I still practice the piano. I'm no genius. It will take a while to get this Mac thing down, and I'll never play piano well enough to stop the dog from barking, but the point is I'm continuing to grow and expand my experiences, knowledge, and expertise.

Look at the people in your company or in your circle of friends. Why do some succeed and others seem to stagnate? Why do some move to higher and higher levels of achievement, while others stay at the same place for years at a time?

Many people blame the system, the company, or their boss. They blame society, their upbringing, or their past. But a lifetime plan for growth can break through barriers and can overcome nearly any obstacle in your life.

Learning is not compulsory . . . neither is survival.
—W. EDWARDS DEMING, MANAGEMENT CONSULTANT

FOUR SIGNS OF STAGNANT GROWTH

1. You lack influence.

You should begin a plan for personal growth immediately if you find you're not influencing decisions, directions, or people. Are friends asking for your advice and then actually listening to you? Do coworkers and associates care about your opinion? Lack of influence is the first sign of stagnant growth. If you're not bringing new ideas and information to the table on a regular basis, people will start to look elsewhere, and you will soon be marginalized within the company.

» GROWTH-ORIENTED ORGANIZATIONS REQUIRE
GROWTH-ORIENTED LEADERSHIP.

It's been said that today business moves at the speed of change. New ideas, technology, leadership techniques, financial models, sales principles, and ways to communicate are being discussed, evaluated, and tested. Company leadership is looking for men and women who aren't just automatons. They're looking for original thinkers, people who go beyond the normal workplace interactions and find new solutions.

Become the go-to guy when it comes to answers and ideas. Be the person who knows how to find new information and who can provide innovative insights and perspectives.

How do you find those ideas?

First, learn where the best ideas in your business come from and spend more time there. I'm not talking about glancing at your monthly trade magazine—it's much more than that. Start with cross-pollinating. Bees spend their lives moving from flower to flower, taking the pollen from one source to another.

What happens?

Growth! Because bees are spreading the pollen around the garden, more flowers start growing, and it becomes a more beautiful place. In life, cross-pollinating means finding information from multiple sources and spreading it out in different ways to different people.

In other words—start looking for answers in unexpected places.

For instance, finding answers to the challenges my media clients face often takes me to history books, computer manuals, magazines on acting, or leadership studies. When faced with a management challenge, I'll often study the lives of military generals and learn about the decisions they made on the battlefield.

Station M

In learning about change, one of the first places I looked was the life of British stage magician Jasper Maskelyne. In 1983, I read David Fisher's remarkable book on Maskelyne's life—*The War Magician*. Maskelyne came from a long line of stage magicians in Britain. When World War II began, his career was at its peak. As he thought about the war effort from a magician's perspective, he realized there were areas he could contribute. Although he was past the normal age for soldiers, he closed up his show and signed up as a private in the British army.

His first personal battle was to convince the military leadership that his ideas would work. Most of the generals were great students of war and had studied it all their lives, so for a *magician*, of all people, to tell them how to approach war from a new perspective was bold, but Maskelyne persisted and managed to get himself and his team into the camouflage department.

The rest is history. Fisher tells the amazing story of how the magician was sent to North Africa, where he used his skills against the Germans to conduct one of the strangest and most bizarre campaigns in the history of warfare.

Using his unusual magical skills, he made the Suez Canal disappear, moved Alexandria Harbor, turned tanks into broken-down trucks, created a shadow army, launched a phantom fleet of submarines, and made the enemy think they were facing a seven-hundred-foot battleship. His team used their inventiveness to create escape kits for prisoners of war, build a mini-submarine that sank a cargo ship, and perfect a special fire-retardant paste that saved the lives of hundreds of fliers.

Jasper Maskelyne spent his whole life trying to change the thinking of people who were hopelessly stuck with an old paradigm. As a master of illusion, his job was to convince people of the impossible and to make the visible, invisible. He had to change the thinking of the public, military generals, and finally, the Nazi army in North Africa.

Keep in mind, he wasn't a military man. When the war started, he had no experience in military affairs and didn't know the first thing about life in the army. But he understood the power of growth and was willing to learn. He established the legendary Station "M"—with the "M" standing for "magic"— where he created a top-secret department building illusions that were used in the global war effort. His work was so important that Hitler's Gestapo added his name to their infamous "Black List," where a price was put on his head. He was so inventive that the Allies kept his illusions in a secret file until nearly forty years after the war.

As a result, after the war he retired at the rank of major and served in sixteen countries, including India, Burma, Malaya, and the Balkans.

Maskelyne understood the power of change—especially the importance of personal growth. He spent his entire life learning, and when he finally died in Kenya in 1973, he had played a significant part in the Allied victory in World War II, created devices that would continue to be used for decades to come, worked for the Kenyan police during the Mau Mau uprising of the 1950s, and managed the Kenyan National Theater. From stage magic to military victory, inventions, police work, and drama, Jasper Maskelyne's life was the story of creativity and personal growth.

I have probably applied more insights from his life to areas like personal change and what I call "crisis creativity" than from any other person.

2. You are not being promoted.

The second indicator of the need to explore personal growth is that you are not being promoted. In corporate culture, the higher the position, the less "doing" happens and the more "thinking" comes into play. Look at a typical corporate conference room during major meetings. The foot soldiers of the company bring in their laptops, briefcases, and sometimes boxes of files, but the president rarely comes into the room holding anything at all.

Why? The president isn't hired to run a computer, keep a schedule, or manage files. He's hired because of the power of his ideas.

Promotions generally go to the men and women who exhibit extraordinary growth, because companies want people in leadership who simply have the best ideas.

Start generating new ideas, and see how quickly you get noticed.

3. You have lost interest in your job.

The third indicator of the need for growth is that you have lost interest in your job or career. Most people think this comes from being in one job too long, going through a midlife crisis, or even the need for some other type of major life change.

> » MOST PEOPLE LOSE INTEREST IN THEIR JOBS BECAUSE THEY LOSE INTEREST IN GROWING.

Look at the people who have the highest levels of intensity and creativity. Generally they are people who are the most passionate about their chosen industry or field. They don't care about the specifics of their job as much as they care about the "big picture" of their field.

I have a friend who teaches film at a university. Although he's quite good at teaching students, grading papers, and setting up classes, his real passion is the movies. He can discuss major films, cultural issues, and the lives of great filmmakers for hours. His daily job is the normal routine of teaching and running a classroom. But his great passion is the subject he teaches. He'll never get tired of teaching or the people he works with, because his life is filled with passion.

Sure, you may get tired of office politics, company forms, office routine, or dealing with clients. I would have to say that, for most of us, the routine aspects of any job can get pretty tedious. But when you're on a personal arc of growth, your passion becomes so much greater. When others are getting bogged down in daily routine, growing people are swinging for a much farther fence. These are people who are growing, learning, and expanding their experience—people who never lose interest in their work.

Overcome your daily routine with a passionate journey of personal growth. Spend as much time expanding your knowledge and experience as you spend on the mundane, and see if your interest levels and excitement don't change for the better.

4. You don't enjoy your coworkers and associates.

A fourth sign is that you don't enjoy your coworkers and associates. One of the most difficult frustrations in the workplace is the (often sudden) feeling that you're growing tired of your coworkers. In most cases, this is another symptom of lack of growth, and it has much to do with the first issue of influence. When you're the go-to person, everyone at work seeks you out. They want your advice and expertise on a myriad of issues and concerns. But when you stop growing, the focus shifts to someone else. Personal growth keeps you focused on people and keeps them focused on you.

*Learning is not attained by chance, it must be sought
for with ardor and attended to with diligence.*
—ABIGAIL ADAMS, FIRST LADY

A life of continual growth is a deliberate plan that requires real effort but can be accomplished by anyone with a sincere desire to expand his or her knowledge and experience.

Where do you start? First, set aside thirty minutes to an hour each day for personal growth. Find the same location if possible—at the office or at home—and dedicate a certain time for pursuing this goal. You might like to get up a little earlier in the morning or do it on your lunch hour, or perhaps it would be more convenient right before bedtime. The time and place don't matter—the important thing is that you stick to it. As I mentioned before, I would encourage you to find the optimum part of the day for your best work. Perhaps you're like me and find that the morning hours are the best time of your day. Other people are afternoon people, and some prefer "rock star hours" late at night.

I pursue growth at two levels: the business level and the leadership level. At the business level, I make it a point to stay up-to-date with my particular industry. You don't have to know everything that goes on in your business, but keeping a working knowledge of the latest breakthroughs, news, and information is vital. To accomplish this, I keep a stack of trade magazines and publications next to my desk. Whenever I have any time to myself—in a doctor's waiting room, on a plane, in a hotel, or waiting for an appointment, I'll pick up a magazine and go through it. This isn't in-depth reading, and it has more to do with "skimming" to look for trends, new ideas, and news. A well-designed RSS strategy is powerful as well. RSS allows you to scan multiple news sources, magazines, and blogs in a remarkably short time. In my case, I set up multiple RSS feeds on different subjects, so I can easily scan the latest information based on different areas of interest.

At the leadership level, I focus on publications and information that help me understand the bigger-picture issues, like vision, spirituality, motivation, and the greater business landscape. All of these ideas are poured into my online blog at philcooke.com.

This is also the fuel for my public speaking. Whether I'm conducting a small workshop or speaking at a major corporate event or conference, the time I spend at the leadership level of growth is a critical part of that preparation.

This category of growth is what drives me on a deep, personal level. This is the time I spend in private spiritual development, personal prayer, and reflection. This level is vital for me to confront my day with confidence, and when I can't do it because of travel or other challenges, I can sense it in my performance, my relationships, and the quality of my work.

Only the curious will learn and only the resolute overcome
the obstacles to learning. The quest quotient has always
excited me more than the intelligence quotient.
—EUGENE S. WILSON, AMHERST COLLEGE

An important thing to realize about personal growth is that it's not about intelligence. One of the biggest complaints I receive about personal growth is that people feel they're not strong enough readers or don't have the level of intelligence they think is required. But it's not about intelligence at all—it's about determination and curiosity.

Consider it a challenge, and if you're ready to answer the challenge, the best will come out of you.

Growth is also the key to mastering your career or calling. There's a great advertising story about shooting a soft drink commercial with Hall of Fame basketball star Larry Bird. The scene called for Larry to shoot a basket and miss the shot. But the scene had to be filmed more than seven times because he was such a great shot that even when he tried to miss, he couldn't help shooting the ball through the basket! At Larry Bird's level of mastery, it's difficult to be anything but excellent.

Peter Brook is a brilliant theatrical director, one of the great giants of worldwide theater. His groundbreaking productions have transformed the art, and his troupe of actors has traveled the world, changing people's perspectives on theatrical presentations. He founded the International Centre of Theatre Research in Paris in 1971 and understands more than most the central role that "challenge" plays in breaking through to the next level. In Margaret Croyden's book *Conversations with Peter Brook*, Brook stated:

No man reveals his depth, or his truth, without a challenge. This is why freedom, if it's weakly conceived, like the freedom of doing your own thing, is always feeble in its result. If you put a man against a mountain, he'll climb it. If you give a man freedom in the face of a challenge, he will use his freedom to wrestle with the challenge. And between freedom and challenge, something powerful comes out. Give a man freedom and no challenge, and the freedom will just peter out. Where acting, directing, writing are concerned, where the creation of plays is concerned, if the actor is given a great part—Oedipus, Prometheus, Hamlet, or Lear—the incredible challenge of doing this will bring the best out of the man. I've seen actors transformed in the course of a season through playing Hamlet. Because the challenge to the imagination, to the spirit, to the emotions of having to understand Hamlet turns the man inside out, and challenges him to give his best.

The challenge of personal growth will transform your life, and like ripples in a pond, it will impact those around you. From time to time, I'll meet people who say, "I'll never forget what you said at last year's industry conference. It was such a challenge for me, I went back and changed everything about the way our organization does business." The power of one speech, one magazine article, or one book can have an impact far greater than we realize.

Chances are you have something inside you that won't be let out without being challenged. Writer Doris Lessing said, "That is what learning is. You suddenly understand something you've understood all your life, but in a new way." Learning isn't just about finding out new things, it's about opening up what's already inside you. In writing this book, I've found myself writing about issues that didn't come through research or through my conscious memory. I've written many things that I didn't even realize I knew. The challenge of writing brought up amazing things from my subconscious that I've learned over the years but that were deep inside me.

That's why growth isn't really about intelligence—it's about the challenge. When you read, listen to podcasts, attend seminars and workshops, participate in a study group, or engage with a mentor, you're discussing, arguing, thinking, reflecting—all the things that expand your horizons and give birth to new ideas and perspectives.

> *The least of learning is done in the classrooms.*
> —THOMAS MERTON, CATHOLIC WRITER AND TEACHER

Realize that growth is all around you. I learn as much about change from an opera as I do from a textbook. Sitting on a plane just last week, I met a man who produces live events at major theme parks. I grilled him about what's popular today, where the technology is going, what challenges he faces, and what direction the industry is heading. Others might have politely said hello and then stared out the window, but I was endlessly fascinated by his expertise, and we talked for about three straight hours.

One of my close friends is the principal of the local high school. Learning how he interacts with students, works with diverse ethnic groups on campus, and provides a vision for the teaching staff is endlessly fascinating to me. I'll never teach at a high school, but understanding how he leads that institution can help me with my business.

Another close friend is a veteran Broadway actor. At my last birthday party (after roasting me), he became serious for a moment and said that one of the best things I've done for him is to help him challenge some of his prejudices. I realized that he's done the same thing for me. We all have prejudices about how we do things, how we think, or how we do business, and it's fascinating that two people from two different backgrounds and businesses could help each other grow in that area.

> *Making a wrong decision is understandable.*
> *Refusing to search continually for learning is not.*
> —PHILIP CROSBY, MANAGEMENT EXPERT

Jolt your brain by planning a life of personal growth. Set aside time for reading, listening to great teachers, and personal reflection. Attend conferences and seminars. Develop a relationship with a mentor. Make an appointment with someone who can help you grow. Engage with people who make you think and who force you to challenge your prejudices and opinions.

Your ability to change your life and impact the world lies in direct proportion to your willingness to learn, expand your thinking, and grow.

CREATIVITY

The *Real* Wonder Drug

Creativity is a drug I cannot live without.
—CECIL B. DEMILLE, MOVIE PRODUCER

A hunch is creativity trying to tell you something.
—AUTHOR UNKNOWN

I had been asked to consult with a major national nonprofit organization that was highly involved in the media. They published a monthly magazine, created a website, and even produced a television program. I immediately reviewed their work and realized it had some serious problems. The style of most of their print and video work was old-fashioned and out of touch, their video techniques were dated, and creativity was, frankly, nonexistent.

I wanted to get to the heart of the matter, so I asked for a meeting with the creative staff. They filed into the room—graphic artists, writers, designers, producers, directors. I spoke for a few minutes about what I had seen in their work, my vision for where the organization could go, and then opened it up for discussion.

They started politely—they *always* start politely—but it didn't take long for their frustrations to vent. It was like pulling a sheet off their problems so we could all see just how ugly it was under there. I wrote down a list of all the reasons they felt that their work wasn't more creative. Since that meeting, the same list has been consistently true with nearly every organization with which I've worked. There are different challenges in many organizations, but the list I wrote down that day has become a guide as I work with other creative teams.

Here's the list of reasons (starting with the most serious) they felt they weren't more creative:

1. We've always done it this way.
2. We're not encouraged to be creative.
3. The organization doesn't foster an attitude of creativity.
4. There are too many rules and sacred cows in the organization that restrict our thinking.
5. We're just not talented enough.

I'll bet that at least one or more of those reasons for a lack of creativity can be found at any organization that's struggling with innovation and creative thinking. They create obstacles to productivity, form barriers to originality, and put the brakes on momentum. I believe every organization and every person can benefit from more creative thinking, but to make that happen, we must first remove the barriers.

Creativity can solve almost any problem. The creative act,
the defeat of habit by originality, overcomes everything.
—GEORGE LOIS, ADVERTISING EXECUTIVE

Let's look at each of those issues and see how you can change your thinking about creativity.

1. WE'VE ALWAYS DONE IT THIS WAY.

No question, this is the single most frustrating sentence in the English language. I hear it over and over, to the point that I've almost begun to ignore it. When you hear someone say, "We've always done it this way," know that he or she is on creative life support. If Dante had written his classic epic poem *Inferno* on creativity, these would be the people in the lowest possible level of hell.

"We've always done it this way" people are usually people who have long ago stopped really thinking and have just become automatons. They are putting in their time, waiting for a check, and going home at the end of the day without thinking, reflecting, or even considering change.

If you're one of these people, forgive me for being so harsh, but it's time you woke up and started looking around at life. Routine is the cancer of creativity. Doing *anything* simply because it was done that way before is not only wrong thinking, it's bad business.

If someone does business the same way every day, that routine is opening that individual up to mistakes because, chances are, the habit has caused him to lose the ability to think critically and question his methods.

If you're doing your job the same way as always, then you're probably already behind. The changing nature of business is making routine approaches to anything a thing of the past.

Creative thinking coach Tom Monahan said, "The information age is now the imagination age." Creativity has pervaded every area of our lives, and to be successful both personally and in business, we need to put away our past fears and embrace a future filled with creativity and innovation.

Tom Kelley, general manager of IDEO, one of the most creative product design firms on the planet, wrote in *The Art of Innovation*: "The biggest single trend that we've observed is the growing acknowledgment of innovation as a centerpiece of corporate strategies and initiatives. What's more, we've noticed that the more senior the executives, the more likely they are to frame their companies' needs in the context of innovation" (3).

Business writer Gary Hamel responded with an interesting but challenging prediction: "Out there in some garage is an entrepreneur who's forging a bullet with your company's name on it. You've got one option now—to shoot first. You've got to out-innovate the innovators."

There is no other choice, in either our personal lives or in our business lives. This is the age of innovation and imagination, and the old ways just don't work anymore.

It *doesn't matter* that we've always done it this way.
It *doesn't matter* that it's always been company policy.
It *doesn't matter* that it's the way the boss likes it.

Organizations are being outthought, outsold, outproduced, and outmanned because their people are stuck thinking they've "always done it this way." Until we can change that thinking, those companies will always be on the losing end of innovation.

How do we get past that thinking?

Start asking questions about everything. Stop taking anything at face value and question policies, techniques, forms, rules, paperwork—anything that has become routine. Why do we do that? Is it even necessary? Can we do it better? On the farm of success, there are no sacred cows. Which leads me to the second issue on the list.

2. WE'RE NOT ENCOURAGED TO BE CREATIVE.

Encouragement is the oxygen of creativity. No individual can creatively function long in an atmosphere where people are taken for granted, go unrewarded, or are ignored. When you encourage and reward people, you're fanning the flames of creativity.

One of the workshops I led recently at a national conference was called "How to Be Creative in a Non-Creative Environment." I have to admit it was depressing to even think there was a need for such a workshop, but the truth is, many very creative individuals suffer by working in companies that don't value innovation. One of my first admonitions at the workshop was: "Get out!" Get out of companies that don't value your gifts and talents. Someone told me: "Go where you are celebrated, not just tolerated." Find a place where your creativity is not only welcomed but also encouraged and rewarded.

If you're in a leadership position, begin today to encourage every person on your staff—especially those who are particularly creative. Which leads me to number three.

3. THE ORGANIZATION DOESN'T FOSTER AN ATTITUDE OF CREATIVITY.

During my meeting with the organization that helped me create this list, I was shocked at the number of rules throughout the building. There were rules for what you could hang on the wall, how you could paint your office, what you could have on your desk, how to dress, and where you could eat.

The truth is, the leaders of the organization weren't bad people; in fact, it was just the opposite—these were wonderful leaders with a deep concern for their employees. They genuinely believed the office should have a uniform, professional look. They didn't realize that the right atmosphere enhances performance, creativity, and innovation.

Since that meeting we've talked the organization's leadership into letting people create their own workspaces and hang whatever inspires them on the wall. We relaxed the dress code and allowed employees to express their individuality. We've even adjusted the work schedule so people can define their own work hours for maximum productivity.

Understand, the transition was done under supervision so it wouldn't descend into pure chaos. Leadership was nervous at first, but now the morale, enthusiasm, and productivity have all surged to levels they had never experienced before.

Today that organization is a place where creativity happens and employees are allowed to question and be more innovative. It's a different atmosphere, and you can sense it the minute you walk in the door.

How do you change the atmosphere in your organization? First, schedule a meeting with your leadership team. I suggest the meeting be held off-site, perhaps at a resort or casual location. Get them away from phones, interruptions, and the pressure of the workplace.

Second, make your own list of what impedes creativity and innovation at your company. Make sure they understand that all restrictions are off and they shouldn't be afraid to be open and honest. A truly open and inventive atmosphere will never happen unless employees know they won't be penalized for their honesty. Make the list and discuss each point. And if you're in a leadership position, be ready for some criticism. Very often, poor innovation is a result of mismanagement, and you may be made to feel that you're partly responsible. Be man or woman enough to take the heat and make the changes you need to make, personally and corporately.

Finally, translate the list into practical reality, which brings us to number four.

4. THERE ARE TOO MANY RULES AND SACRED COWS IN THE ORGANIZATION THAT RESTRICT OUR THINKING.

Here's where the rubber meets the road. Organizational leadership has to be willing to put their money where their mouth is. You have to make the list concrete, to make the necessary policy changes to make original thinking a priority. For instance, in our case, our first plan of attack was to provide more creative tools for the employees. In the past, certain software programs, equipment requests, and other tools were deemed too expensive or unnecessary. But for creative people, the right digital tools and software become essential. Just approving those purchases made a huge difference in employee morale.

So don't think creativity is just about thinking. In today's marketplace, Michelangelo would use the latest software, Rembrandt would want the new mobile device, and Leonardo da Vinci would no doubt demand a bigger video screen. Art historians tell us that the great masters of the past all used the best equipment and went to extraordinary lengths to find the finest materials for their paints, brushes, and canvas. They would be no different today.

- Make sure your people have the right tools for maximum creativity.
- Change the rules. Rethink policies. Question everything.

I'll admit this isn't always easy. In many organizations, certain rules and policies have been in place for decades, and changing them is similar to adding an amendment to the Constitution.

But change them you must.

When Alexander the Great visited Diogenes and asked whether
he could do anything for the famed teacher, Diogenes replied:
"Only stand out of my light." Perhaps some day we shall know
how to heighten creativity. Until then, one of the best things
we can do for creative men and women is to stand out of their light.
—JOHN W. GARDNER, NOVELIST AND WRITING TEACHER

One of the most damaging sacred cows in organizations is basing employee status on seniority rather than talent. Yes, loyalty is important, but some of the most loyal employees I've ever met are loyal because of selfishness. They project loyalty to keep their jobs, retain their benefits, or hold on to their authority. Real loyalty is about innovation, original thinking, and helping the company get to the next level.

> » **NEVER MISTAKE LOYALTY FOR COMPETENCE OR VALUE. SOME OF YOUR MOST LOYAL EMPLOYEES ARE THE LEAST VALUABLE TO YOUR ORGANIZATION.**

Everyone has intrinsic value. Every person has worth and is important. But a great leader always knows the people who bring the most value to the organization. Those are the people to be developed, trained, and cultivated.

Create an atmosphere of original thinking and you'll have more loyalty than you'll know what to do with. Most companies are so ignorant of how to develop an environment of innovation that if you do it, you'll have people coming from every direction to work with you.

5. WE'RE JUST NOT TALENTED ENOUGH.

I've put this last on the list because of the most frequently asked question at workshops and conferences. People from all walks of life come up to me and say, "I'm just not a creative person, so I'll never be able to do these things." Others ask, "Can I ever be creative?"

All of us were born creative. Find any child and play with him or her for five minutes and you'll see creativity in action. Children can visualize worlds you've never dreamed of and places beyond imagination. The most bizarre fairy tales seem absolutely believable to a child, and there is no limit to the creativity of children.

This is beautifully illustrated in Chris Van Allsburg's classic Christmas book *The Polar Express*. A young boy is beginning to question the existence of Santa Claus, and after a breathtaking Christmas Eve trip to the North Pole on the Polar Express train, he discovers his ability to believe is directly related to his ability to hear a ringing bell on Santa's sleigh. Early on, the skeptical young man can't hear the bells, but as his belief in Santa grows, he slowly begins to hear the bell. When Santa gives him the bell as the first gift of Christmas, he and his sister can clearly hear its beautiful sound—but his parents can't. Later, as he grows up, his sister loses her ability to hear it, as do most of his friends. But because he never stops believing in Santa, he is able to hear the sweet, clear sound of the ringing sleigh bell for the rest of his life.

Creativity is no different. We all start out amazingly creative, but as we grow older, the ringing bell of creative thinking grows softer and softer. There is a difference of opinion about what causes this—the educational system, a growing maturity, the sense that we're "supposed" to be more rational as we grow up, taking on adult responsibilities—whatever it is, it's a tragic loss.

Creativity is allowing yourself to make mistakes.
Art is knowing which ones to keep.
—SCOTT ADAMS, CREATOR OF *DILBERT*

Granted, some people are more creative than others. Just as some people are stronger, faster, or smarter than the rest, some people seem to be born with more creativity. But the fact is, all of us were born creative, and we can all grow in creativity.

How?

Don't be afraid to start with a blank page.

Every great idea started from nothing, but most people can't move past a blank page. Start making notes or drawing pictures—dancer and choreographer Twyla Tharp calls it "scratching." Look for bits and pieces of ideas in any number of places—reading, watching, thinking, reflecting. Find places that "feel" more creative and spend time there. Perhaps it's a museum, a bookstore, or an empty chair in your bedroom. Wherever it is, that's where the creative process can start for you.

Stop worrying about being wrong.

The fear of being wrong is poison for the creative process. Creativity is not about right or wrong. It's about problem solving. Begin thinking in terms of problem solving and you'll master the art of creative thinking.

Understand that creativity is not a state of being.

Creativity is about action. You can't "be creative." Don't believe me? Okay, try it. Try "being creative." Any luck? I didn't think so. Creativity is the process of *doing*, and that act of doing is solving problems. Look at the list of great creative people—writers, artists, engineers, software designers, advertising executives, animators, and many more—they all were concerned about solving a problem, and they solved it with their work. A novel about injustice, a software program that helps create better photos, the painted ceiling of a chapel, an advertisement that sells juice. Creativity isn't about a state of being, it's about an end result.

That understanding alone will free you to instantly take your original thinking to a higher level.

> *The best way to get a good idea is to get a lot of ideas.*
> —LINUS PAULING, SCIENTIST AND HUMANITARIAN

Learn the art of brainstorming.

When I teach brainstorming techniques at workshops, my greatest obstacle is people who think they already know how to do it. Most people assume brainstorming is just getting a lot of people into a room and kicking around some ideas.

Wrong.

Effective brainstorming is a skill, just like good writing. Here are some tips to help you increase the productivity of your brainstorming sessions.

Create the right atmosphere.

Find a place with no distractions. I suggest a location away from the office, but that's not necessary. In fact, at a resort or similar location, the "fun factor" may be too much of a distraction. I have difficulty being productive when there are windows in the room. Likewise, sometimes it's best to find a brainstorming location with few other options so the team will stay focused on the goal. Just make sure it's a relaxed atmosphere where original thinking can flourish. Don't allow interruptions, and make sure everyone knows what the session is about so your team can be thinking about the issues ahead of time. Also, make sure the session is well supplied—paper, markers, chart paper, and don't forget coffee, cookies, water, or other refreshments.

Don't include too many people.

Jeff Bezos, founder of Amazon.com, says that the best sessions have no more people than you can feed with two pizzas. When you allow too many people into the session, it becomes unwieldy, unfocused, and hard to manage. Everyone will want to be involved, but you have to restrict it to the most pertinent people involved in the particular issue. I like to limit the session to six people if possible, and I rarely make it more than ten. Sometimes more can work, depending on the problem to be solved, but generally, keep the numbers lower.

Have lots of ideas.

Brainstorming is about volume. Make sure everyone knows there are no limits, no boundaries, not even budget constraints. The purpose is to get everything out on the table. You never know what your next big idea is, so at this point, don't limit yourself to what you think is possible or affordable. I suggest you have someone keep a list of the ideas and number them. That will help later when you go back to review, and it gives you some sense of how many ideas are being generated. One good suggestion is to hang poster paper or butcher paper on the walls and have people randomly write or draw their ideas on the paper. It keeps people moving, ideas pumping, and momentum marching forward.

No criticism allowed.

In the initial stages of brainstorming, it's not about how good an idea is or whether or not it will work. It's about getting the ideas on the table. So the most important rule of a good session is *no criticism*. If someone tosses out an idea and you call it stupid or unworkable, chances are, it will be the last idea you get from that person. And who knows? His or her next idea may have been the big one that saved the company. Don't let anyone criticize an idea or a person. Criticism is probably the biggest idea killer than can infect a brainstorming session.

Keep it to an hour or so.

Someone once asked film director Alfred Hitchcock, "What's the perfect length for a movie?" His response: "The length of a film should be directly related to the endurance of the human bladder."

The same holds true for brainstorming sessions. I've noticed that after an hour, people start getting restless and off track. Keep the sessions to an hour and you'll get the best out of people. In special brainstorming sessions, you can go longer, but I would provide long breaks at the top of each hour. Brainstorming is mental, but our minds are also connected to our bodies, and our bodies scream for breaks. Get up, walk around, get some coffee, or go outside.

The fact is, if you're having brainstorming sessions on a regular basis, an hour is all you need. Get into a regular habit of brainstorming with your key people and you'll find that you become a finely tuned idea machine. Speaking of fine tuning—

Fine-tune the ideas.

At some point, it's time to take the hopefully huge list of ideas and edit them to the best idea. This isn't easy, but it is necessary. Start with the obvious ideas that can't work because of budget, time schedule, or lack of resources. If someone suggested opening your sales conference with the Victoria's Secret models, that might be out of your price range. Having your marketing retreat on top of Mount Everest might be a bit tough as well. Make your first edits on the things that stand out.

Next, pull ideas that are probably good but won't solve the particular problem you're facing. Some great ideas are ahead of their time. Fine. Put them in your files and pull them out next year.

In the end, you should have your list of real, practical ideas that could work. It may be good to let that list gel over time. Perhaps you bring the team back in a week to discuss which of those ideas will work best. If you've developed a great team, then politics and ownership of ideas shouldn't be a problem. A great team knows it's not about individual stars, and one person shouldn't campaign for an idea just because it was his or hers. Develop a team that values the best ideas and will work to fine-tune the list until you all agree on the best possible solution.

Follow the path of the unsafe, independent thinker. Expose your ideas to the dangers of controversy. Speak your mind and fear less the label of "crackpot" than the stigma of conformity. And on issues that seem important to you, stand up and be counted at any cost.
—THOMAS J. WATSON, FOUNDER OF IBM

Commit to a life of creativity and original thinking. Dress differently, drive home an unusual way, look at your job from a new perspective, stop taking people and things for granted. A life of creativity is a wonderful world where you'll encounter new possibilities and see the world from a distinctive viewpoint. Just as in many other areas of change, some people will be upset with you. Lots of people out there hate creative thinking. They don't like change, and therefore originality is something they are uncomfortable with and shun. Many people in corporate leadership don't like their policies questioned or their dictates doubted.

But the results of original thinking cannot be doubted, questioned, or criticized.

Tom Kelley, in the closing of *The Art of Innovation* (see p. 87 here), wrote:

Try it yourself. Innovation isn't about perfection. You've got to shank a few before your swing smooths out. Get out there and observe the market, your customers, and products. Brainstorm like crazy and prototype in bursts. You know the drill. The next time you're knee deep in a challenging project, don't forget the true spirit of innovation. That's right. Have some serious fun. (297)

Perhaps the best-selling point for creative thinking is fun. It makes work seem like a playground and can transform your attitude toward your job and your business. Innovation can build teams of top performers and create a corporate atmosphere of excitement, enthusiasm, and loyalty.

It works in your personal life as well. When you can view every aspect of your life as a creative opportunity, the mundane becomes a compelling adventure and you'll begin to see everything in a new light.

The classic advertisements for Apple computer said it best: "Think Different."

EMBRACE AMBIGUITY

Appreciating the Mystery of Life

*The test of a first-rate intelligence is the ability
to hold two opposed ideas in the mind at the same time,
and still retain the ability to function.*
—F. SCOTT FITZGERALD, NOVELIST

*If you really want something in life, you have to work for it.
Now, quiet! They're about to announce the lottery numbers.*
—HOMER SIMPSON

I like to toss out provocative thoughts on Twitter and Facebook just to see the reaction. It often leads to fascinating discussions, but more than anything I've noticed just how black-and-white some people can be. They want clear and simple answers to everything and can't tolerate shades of gray. But the truth is, we don't have answers for a lot that happens in the world.

Why does one family experience tragedy and another doesn't? Why does a company fail in spite of a great product? Why is there so much need in the world? Why can't I accomplish my dream?

One of the hallmarks of the modern mind—especially during the last hundred years—was certainty. The rise of modern science made us believe that everything can be proven given enough time, and in the age of modernity, we came to see our world as something measurable, concrete, and exact. But we've discovered that life isn't as exact as we thought. In our age of "scientism," we put our faith in science and considered religious belief to be primitive and foolish. We discovered that, while science matters enormously, it doesn't necessarily hold the promise we thought it did. Marriages still fail, rates of violence and crime have not fallen, and wars still exist.

Life is wonderful, but it is also quite messy.

As a pastor's son, I attended more funerals by age twelve than most people attend in a lifetime. My dad conducted funerals for children, teenagers, young adults—many people who had no reason to die and every reason to live.

> *Again I saw that . . . the race is not to the swift . . . nor favor to the skillful; but time and chance happen to them all.*
> —ECCLESIASTES 9:11 NRSV

If we are to understand *real* change, we have to accept the mystery of life, realize that it's not always fair and that we don't have all the answers. If post-modern thought can help us, this is perhaps its strongest argument. Life is not necessarily about certainty, being right, or finding all the answers.

In a disrupted world, the secret to life is about asking the right questions.

From the beginning, we have been creatures of choice. We are not ruled by instincts, robotic instructions, or programming. We have a choice—but within that choice is the great paradox.

Choice means . . .

- we are free to do evil as well as good.
- we live in a world where birth, life, and growth are balanced by decay, disease, and destruction.
- the responsibility to do the right thing—not the license to do what we please.
- true redemption is in the struggle of life.
- ambiguity.

Listen to the evening news for very long and you'll see the parade of people demanding "rights" for everything you can possibly imagine. On camera these people are quick to talk about *rights*, but not so quick to talk about *responsibilities*. Understanding ambiguity is to take responsibility for our own lives in spite of what happens to us. Accepting ambiguity may be our greatest act of faith.

Bookstores are filled with books providing easy answers. Go to the self-help or business section and you'll find a multitude of titles such as *The Three Easy Steps to Financial Success, Living at Your Best, Successful Families,* or *The Secrets of a Strong Marriage.* I've read most of those type of books over the years, and I have to admit that I'm still not as financially secure as I'd like, I could still be living better, my family does dumb things, and my wife and I continue to have our spats. I've discovered the search for easy answers is a futile effort that usually leads to failure.

Yes, much of the information in these books is terrific. Many of the facts are right-on, and they include things that can really help people. But the truth is, life isn't about finding easy answers—life is about asking the right questions.

When you can get away from your obsessive search for effortless answers to the problems you face, you'll begin to understand a much bigger picture.

» LIFE DOESN'T ALWAYS MAKE SENSE.

Sometimes no matter how hard we work, the project still fails. No matter how hard we try, our spouses still file for divorce. And no matter how much we intervene, a child still experiments with drugs or alcohol.

I watched the TV news last night as a father wept because his thirteen-year-old daughter decided to take the family car on a joyride, lost control, and killed two young children. She came from a good family, she was an excellent student, and her parents loved her and raised her by the book. There was no reason for her impulse, but she did it anyway, and now three families are shattered.

As I looked at that weeping father, I realized there are no easy answers in life.

I saw all the deeds that are done under the sun; and see, all is vanity and a chasing after wind.
—ECCLESIASTES 1:14 NRSV

If you think the Bible is a story of fairy tales for wimps, think again. The Old Testament book of Ecclesiastes was written by a man who had seen everything, been everywhere, and owned as much as any man on the earth. He had enjoyed everything life had to offer, and all he saw was emptiness and vanity. He understood the difference between a life of true understanding and a life devoid of purpose and meaning. It's a book that deals with the reality of living and doesn't hold back or cut corners.

Film critic and professor of theology and culture Robert Johnston wrote in his book *Useless Beauty: Ecclesiastes Through the Lens of Contemporary Film*:

> Medieval Old Testament scholars called Ecclesiastes one of the Bible's "two most dangerous books." (The other was the Song of Songs with its overt sensuality.) Though its trenchant observations on life reveal a fragile joy—a useless beauty—its paragraphs also brim over with a cynicism and even a despair that seem out of place in the Bible's grand narrative. (19)

But at the end of this despair, the writer of Ecclesiastes also offers us hope. He offers real wisdom instead of easy answers. Life is not a manageable project or a test to be taken. We can find small joys every day if we have eyes of faith. We can find meaning if we search for a greater purpose. And perhaps most important, we need to realize that life is a great gift.

In M. Night Shyamalan's movie *Signs*, a Pennsylvania minister has lost his faith and abandoned his calling because of the senseless death of his wife. But as the story unfolds, he discovers fragments of meaning in normally inconsequential events. Things others don't notice begin to have enormous meaning for this former pastor. The Bible says in 1 Corinthinans 13:12 that now we see in part, and for him, the parts begin to make sense. Finally, as he is able to set aside his bitterness and anger, he begins to piece together the meaning and once again discover his faith.

So what can we make of this idea of ambiguity? How can we face a world without all the answers when we have deep questions and yearnings that we don't understand?

Writer Peter Block suggests that we should stop looking for simple answers and start asking bigger questions. For things that really matter, you'll find the real answer deep inside the question. It's interesting that when the people of the New Testament asked Jesus questions, he turned right back to them with another question. Great teachers and philosophers throughout history have done the same thing.

These teachers understood the power of questions and how questions can be the key to real understanding. Life is complicated. Life is difficult. Life is not so neat. The obvious answers we're looking for aren't always in front of our noses.

» STOP WAITING TO FINISH.

Life is about the journey, not the destination. It sounds trite and clichéd, but its real meaning is more powerful than we can imagine. It's written on cute motivational posters, but we ignore its real power. Stop waiting to arrive. As a young man, I spent most of my life "waiting to finish." Driving in the car on summer vacation, I couldn't wait to get there; in school, I couldn't wait to get out of class; at work, I couldn't wait to finish the project. Then one day I realized that I've spent most of my life waiting for something and never enjoying the process. I had missed most of life's greatest moments in anticipation of something else.

Nothing reveals that frustration as much as watching your children grow. Our daughters are grown, and it's amazing to realize that only yesterday they were sitting on my lap telling me what they wanted for Christmas. Kathleen and I watch home videos and wish we could go back, just for a day. They grew up so fast, and I wish I had been in the moment and relished those early days a little more.

My life is here and now. My family is here and now. My marriage is here and now. My career is here and now. The journey happens every day.

Dr. Larry Poland, founder of Mastermedia International in Hollywood, puts it this way: "Stop rowing and start sailing." Dr. Poland describes most people as struggling against the wind, rowing, giving it their best but wearing themselves out in the process. They want to control their direction and force the boat to go a particular way.

Experienced sailors know that if they just relax a little, they can steer but let the wind do the real work. You might not go in the exact direction you prefer, and you might even wander off course a little. But knowing how to steer will still take you to the same place and allow you to enjoy the trip.

Sometimes, like a drowning man, we struggle against the very things that can save us.

Sit back, relax a little, and accept the mystery. Perhaps how you get there doesn't matter quite so much. The writer of Ecclesiastes knew that we all end up at the same destination—dust. The only difference is how we enjoy the journey.

We can either celebrate the mystery and ambiguity of life or spend our years upset, frustrated, angry, and bitter because things don't always go our way or finish like we wanted. Hospitals are filled with people who have allowed stress to break down their minds and bodies, and in a significant number of cases, it was stress over things that they had no control over.

I can't change the weather, change other people's behavior, or add a single day to my life. So I'm going to focus on things I *can* change and leave the rest to God.

As a believer in God I have to believe that God is in control, and for me to always demand answers is to assume his role. I've decided to sit back and let him be God and let me be me.

THE POWER OF GENEROSITY

Getting More Out of Life by Giving It Away

When you become detached mentally from yourself and concentrate on helping other people with their difficulties, you will be able to cope with your own more effectively. Somehow, the act of self-giving is a personal power-releasing factor.

—NORMAN VINCENT PEALE

Generosity with strings is not generosity; it is a deal.

—MARYA MANNES, WRITER AND CRITIC

Early in my career, I produced an infomercial program for a client in Hollywood. In those days, infomercials were a new type of advertising and usually featured a thirty-minute program designed to sell products such as exercise machines, kitchen tools, or makeup. An old college friend recommended me, and since it was a new style of advertising, I was eager to be part of the project.

Until I met the client.

At first he seemed quite normal. His office was average, and he was located in a nice part of town. His secretary seemed nice enough, and everything about him appeared to indicate that he was a legitimate, effective producer.

But once we started working together, it didn't take long to see that he held on to money with a vise-like grip. I was young and idealistic, so I ignored most of the warning signs, but as the project progressed, I saw that although he talked the talk, when it came to money, keeping it for himself was an obsession.

103

It's one thing to negotiate better prices, but this guy would flatly refuse to pay any price he didn't like. He would never pay for anything in advance, and once someone delivered, he would look for any reason to refuse to pay. In fact, when the entire project was over, he shortchanged me about five thousand dollars. When I asked for the money, he had his lawyers send a letter to intimidate me into walking away.

He was so tight, even his own partner called me later to apologize for his stingy and unprofessional behavior.

He has reaped what he sowed all those years ago. Not long ago, I heard that his clients had grown tired of being nickeled-and-dimed, film crews won't work with him, and investors saw too much money going into his pocket and not enough going into the TV projects. His tight-fisted attitude toward money has finally cost him his career as a producer.

But I also noticed something else.

His stingy attitude toward money extended to everything else in his life. Because he refused to be generous with money, he wasn't generous with his time, his relationships, or his business. As a result, he was a lonely man with few friends and a miserable life.

You cannot live a perfect day without doing something
for someone who will never be able to repay you.
—JOHN WOODEN, UCLA BASKETBALL COACH

The dictionary defines *generosity* as "liberality in giving" or a "willingness to give." Most people think of generosity in terms of financial resources, such as giving to the poor or giving to church or charities. It is certainly that, but the most important thing you can learn about giving is that it's a *lifestyle*.

> » **GIVERS ARE PEOPLE WHO UNDERSTAND THAT MONEY, TIME, LOVE, KNOWLEDGE, AND POSSESSIONS ONLY HAVE VALUE WHEN THEY CAN BE USED TO HELP OTHERS.**

Thousands of years ago, teachers taught about giving and did so in terms of two possibilities. First, give to help others. Second, when you give, it comes back to you many times over.

But how can that be? How can giving something away benefit me?

I had a mentor early in my career who explained it this way: "When your fists are clenched holding something tight, you can't keep them open to receive."

Since working with that stingy producer many years ago, I've deliberately taken another approach. I've made generosity a vital part of our business and actively searched for ways we can help others through our limited financial and production resources. When we produce television programs or commercials—within the capability of our accounting procedures—we try to pay people as quickly as possible. I want them to feel that we value their services and appreciate their commitment to our company. As a result, I've not only seen a rise in the quality of their work, but I've also had freelance crew members and vendors completely rearrange other projects in order to work with us.

We also work with numerous nonprofits, religious ministries, and social service agencies. We donate as much of our time and resources as we can to help them produce high-quality fund-raising and promotional video programming. Even when a client refuses to pay us, we still make a point to pay our employees, crew members, and vendors—even when it hurts.

That attitude and commitment have created tangible benefits for us. When we are in a financial or scheduling bind, our people or vendors don't hesitate to take less money, change schedules, or give far more time and effort than is normally required. They're happy to repay our generosity by giving of themselves and their resources.

Many times we'll approach them with a project we're doing for free for a nonprofit or ministry client, and they're happy to participate without charging because they know we're people of our word, who are generous whenever we can be.

Only those who have learned the power of sincere and selfless
contribution experience life's deepest joy: true fulfillment.
—ANTHONY ROBBINS, MOTIVATIONAL SPEAKER AND TELEVISION PERSONALITY

How can you become a giver?

First, understand it's not about the amount of money. Lots of people will say, "Well, as soon as I get rich, I'll become more generous." But some of the greatest givers I've ever met have the least money. Grandmothers on meager pensions are sending a few dollars a month to help build orphanages. People barely making it are giving financially to help feed the hungry. Retired employees are mentoring younger workers. And single people with few financial resources are spending their evenings working with the homeless or families in need.

No matter where you are financially, you can begin a lifestyle of giving. After all, you have money for dining out, movie tickets, dating, other leisure activities, or a nice car. Chances are, you can find something to give.

Second, money is only the beginning of a lifestyle of giving. What other ways can you help someone in need? There's probably a retired person in your neighborhood who needs help cleaning house, clearing out the gutters, painting, or getting to the doctor. One man was mowing his lawn and decided it would only take a few more minutes to mow his recently widowed neighbor's yard, and that act of generosity has continued for years, saving her thousands of dollars.

What about at the office? Could you spend a few hours a week mentoring a younger employee? Could you give some time to organize a company outreach in the community? What about helping a coworker who's going through a particularly difficult time?

> *No person was ever honored for what he received.*
> *Honor has been the reward for what he gave.*
> —CALVIN COOLIDGE, PRESIDENT OF THE UNITED STATES

Third, take your generosity to a new level. Look around you. Want to make a real difference? Pick an area of interest and it's not difficult to locate an organization working to change that particular area. Energy conservation, drug education and counseling, orphanages, arts programs, voter registration, church-based ministries, day care, literacy programs, youth outreaches, the environment, animal rescue, recycling programs, helping the elderly, global missions, feeding programs, mentoring, minority business consulting, and more. The list is pretty endless, and there are amazing organizations and ministries making a dramatic difference in the world.

But they need your help. Perhaps you can't physically participate, but you can give financially. I know a young female executive who financially supports a charitable ministry building orphanages in Haiti. She's never been to the island, but her monthly check is feeding hundreds of young children and providing them a place to live.

Others want a more hands-on approach. They want to do more than just give money, so they show up to work at soup kitchens, counsel troubled teens, build houses, or work in after-school programs.

Although I prefer personal involvement, it really doesn't matter so much whether you let your money make a difference or give of yourself; the important thing is you're giving back to the community and impacting the lives of people on a regular basis.

Fourth, think in terms of your expertise. I'm astonished at how few people think about using their personal skills and talents to help these organizations, when that approach may be the most significant impact you could possibly have. I recently met a man who had just retired from being the chief financial officer of a Fortune 500 company and was now volunteering at a faith-based organization working for peace in the Middle East. After more than thirty years of financial expertise at the highest levels of corporate America, he is now helping this organization make a major impact through fund-raising and strategic financial planning.

> *There is no greater joy nor greater reward than*
> *to make a fundamental difference in someone's life.*
> —SISTER MARY ROSE MCGREADY

Perhaps you're an advertising executive who could help a local social service agency promote its work or raise money. If you have experience as a builder, you could consider organizations that build low-income housing or help renovate homes for the poor or elderly. If you're a graphic artist, you could design stationery, brochures, logos, and other print materials for charities, churches, or other nonprofit organizations.

A travel agent wanted to help a large charity that was actively involved in building water wells overseas, and he eagerly volunteered to dig wells in poverty-stricken countries. I made the following suggestion: "I'm sure they appreciate the help digging wells, but the fact is, you're not very good at it. On the other hand, you're a great travel agent. Have you ever offered to help book their travel to the various countries?" He thought about it and realized he had never mentioned what he actually did for a living to anyone at the charity. When he finally told the organization's leadership, they were thrilled because travel planning was one of their greatest areas of need. He made the switch and has made a dramatic difference in their travel scheduling, booking, expenses, and the efficiency of their travel needs, saving them thousands of dollars in the process.

Jolt your wallet and your time, and when you do, remember that generosity is more than a onetime event—it's a lifestyle. Build a reputation as a giver and see the incredible harvest that will result. Avenues of change will open to you as you reach out to help others. Never forget that you were born with great personal gifts and abilities. Find ways to use your skills to help those less fortunate, and your efforts will be multiplied.

THE KEY TO PERSONAL CONFIDENCE

Overcoming Fear and Insecurity

Inaction breeds doubt and fear. Action breeds confidence and courage. If you want to conquer fear, do not sit home and think about it. Go out and get busy.

—DALE CARNEGIE

Courage is fear that has said its prayers.

—DOROTHY BERNARD, SILENT FILM STAR

We had just taken off on a flight from Miami, headed to Heathrow Airport in London. We had been filming in Haiti, before the days that all foreign airports had computers, so just getting on an outbound flight had been a nightmare. We'd been up all night before leaving Haiti—haggling with the airline—and after getting bumped from three flights, we spent most of the day in the Miami airport, having our tickets changed and plans rerouted.

About an hour into the flight, I noticed the flight attendants starting to get a little nervous. They seemed to be roaming up and down the aisles with more urgency than normal, with enough intensity to make me sit up and take notice.

That's when the pilot's halting voice came over the intercom: "Ladies and gentlemen, we don't want to alarm you, but Miami flight control has just relayed that they've received a message a bomb might be onboard this flight."

There was immediate silence throughout the cabin. Not the kind of silence created from just an absence of sound, but the kind of silence that feels eerie, like the calm before an impending storm.

The pilot spoke again, this time trying to be a little more encouraging. "Just to be sure, we're going back to Miami because we always take these messages seriously. As a precaution, we're going to dump our fuel over the ocean and then return to the airport."

Interesting what you think about when you face possible death. Even more interesting was watching and listening to the other people on the plane.

Some quietly sobbed, others prayed out loud, but most sat deep in thought. I pulled out a small tape recorder and quietly turned it on, recording the sounds in the cabin. It was an almost mystical moment as people suddenly stopped laughing, reading, or talking, and began looking inward. Were they thinking about their families? Loved ones? Death? The hereafter?

Since that time, I've been detained and questioned while filming during military coups in foreign countries, been threatened on location by insurgents and rebels, crossed rivers filled with piranha, traveled with Bedouins in the deserts, and been so sick deep in the Amazon jungle I would have gladly considered death. But I've never quite experienced the feeling of fear as I did that day flying back to the Miami airport.

> *None but a coward dares to boast that he has never known fear.*
> —FERDINAND FOCH, WWI FRENCH MILITARY GENERAL

Fear is a normal part of living. It keeps us out of trouble, warns us when we're getting into risky situations, and makes us think twice when we get a little too bold for our own good. But excessive fear, like anything else, can hold us back. When fear gets out of control, it can paralyze and destroy.

For millions of people today, certain fears are simmering just below the surface. For most, you'd never know there was any problem at all. We keep them hidden away from public view, and we've mastered the art of disguise and concealment. In fact, some people spend their entire lives refusing to acknowledge these emotions. We spend an enormous amount of emotional effort keeping our insecurities, anxieties, and fears under control, but at a great toll on our emotional well-being.

» IMAGINED FEAR IS JUST AS TERRIFYING AS REAL FEAR.

Neuroscientists at Yale University and New York University discovered that patients who expected to experience an electric shock suffered anxieties similar to those who had a response to a real threat. Researcher Elizabeth Phelps was quoted in a *Psychology Today* article (September 1, 2001): "A lot of our fears and anxieties are learned through communication. If someone tells you to be afraid of a dog, then the brain responds as if you actually were."

In other words, our brains don't know the difference between *real* threats and *imagined* threats, which does much to explain why the National Institute of Mental Health reported that nineteen million Americans suffer from anxiety disorders. Someone who is perfectly safe, but who has a fear of being robbed, suffers just as much as someone living in a situation with a high risk for robbery or someone actually in the act of being robbed.

Because our brains don't discriminate between emotions that are real or imagined, fear can dominate our lives and is just as devastating as physical injury.

For the most part, fear is nothing but an illusion.
When you share it with someone else, it tends to disappear.
—MARILYN BARRICK, PSYCHOLOGIST

According to a 2004 article on "Conquering Our Phobias" in *U.S. News and World Report*, some of the most famous people throughout history suffered from serious fear, many just like those listed above. Napoleon Bonaparte was crippled by ailurophobia, the fear of cats. Queen Elizabeth I is said to have been terrorized by anthophobia, a general fear of flowers, and she particularly feared roses. Howard Hughes was nearly paralyzed by mysophobia, a fear of germs; and Edgar Allen Poe, Harry Houdini, and Adolf Hitler were claustrophobic. Even the father of psychoanalysis, Sigmund Freud, experienced agoraphobia, a fear of crowds and public places.

Although anxiety issues and phobias affect millions of Americans, most of us would deny dealing with any overwhelming fear and rarely consider it a serious problem. But truthfully, many small fears hinder us on our journey toward change, and unless we face them, we'll never fully reach our potential. Perhaps you don't even consider what bothers you a fear. Perhaps it's just a feeling or situation you avoid or leave to others. Whatever it is, the way to overcome the issue is to recognize it as fear and make a decision to change.

WHAT ARE YOU AFRAID OF?

Fear of speaking in public?

Being able to lead discussions, conduct workshops, make effective presentations, and speak to employees is a critical skill required for leadership. Overcome your fear by taking a public speaking class, volunteer to be a discussion leader on your team, or offer to lead the next brainstorming session. I also suggest spending time with people who are good at public communication. Run your questions by them, get their advice, or ask them to coach you in public speaking.

Fear of failure?

This fear is amazingly common in workplaces across America, and it keeps millions of people from achieving their potential. Look closely at the real impact of failure's actual consequences, and you'll often laugh at its power over you. So what if you make a mistake during your presentation? Chances are, no one is going to shoot you. So what if you miss the mark on the project or make an error in your calculations? We all want to be perfect, but the fact is, we're all flawed.

In reality, the irrational fear of failure and refusal to embrace mistakes creates far more mistakes in the long run. When people won't face the possibility of having made errors, they often refuse to have someone else check their work or ask for help reviewing a project. As a result, they make more poor choices and mistakes, which continue to feed their insecurities.

Fear of not being good enough?

My wife grew up in a home where, after the untimely death of her younger brother due to a heart condition, few things she ever did were good enough. Her parents were wonderful people who didn't know better, but they placed expectations on their only daughter that a normal child could rarely fulfill. Her parents held Robby up as the ideal child, and everything Kathleen and her older brother accomplished was compared against the impossible standard of Robby. Growing up, they became all too familiar with lines like:

"Robby would have never done that."

"Everyone loved Robby. He got along with everyone."

"Robby was so much more disciplined than you."

Like many parents in this situation, they weren't intentionally trying to hurt Kathleen or her brother, but they recalled a perfect (if inaccurate) picture in their hearts and minds of their son who had died, and Robby became the ultimate example of the perfect child.

Years of hearing those comments created insecurities in Kathleen, and in spite of the fact that she is an accomplished actress, teacher, wife, mother, and partner in our company, it took her a long time to overcome the fear of not being good enough and a need to compare herself with others.

Just as Kathleen discovered about her life, you *are* good enough. I once heard an old gospel preacher shout, "God didn't create no junk!" He's right. You have talents, gifts, and abilities like no one else on earth.

Like your fingerprint, you are unique, different, and exceptional. It's not about *being as good* as others; it's about *being different* from others. Stop spending so much time comparing yourself to others, and spend your time discovering your unique gifts and talents. You were born for a purpose, and that purpose may be unlike anything you've encountered before.

Fear of not being accepted?

Fear of not being accepted is one of the great causes of loneliness. It's been said that the Internet has made this the most connected generation in history, and yet the loneliest. Tonight millions of people will go home to an empty apartment, eat dinner for one, and climb into bed alone. Even surrounded by a crowd, many people feel completely isolated, like an island in the middle of a vast ocean. Novelist Thomas Wolfe called it the central and inevitable fact of human existence.

The most important key to being accepted is to accept others. When you allow others into your private world, you'll discover that they will often welcome you into theirs.

Insecurity is another critical issue related to fear. Just as my wife has wrestled with insecurities resulting from her past, millions of others experience crippling insecurities that hold them back from reaching their real potential.

Courage is the art of being the only one
who knows you're scared to death.
—HAROLD WILSON, BRITISH PRIME MINISTER

I've been to meetings filled with experts in a particular area with which I was unfamiliar. Looking around the room, I hoped they wouldn't ask me a question or call on me to address an issue, because I knew I'd look like a complete idiot. In a similar way, traveling to other countries might make you a bit insecure—particularly when you don't even speak the language well enough to ask how to find a restroom.

Those types of minor insecurities happen all the time and are a normal part of living.

Many people, however, are trapped in a self-imposed prison of deep insecurity. Insecurities are particularly damaging because they eat at your self-esteem. They destroy your confidence by making you feel stupid, incompetent, or embarrassed. People like this can't be taught, accept honest criticism, or grow. The very thing they often need the most is usually the last thing they are willing to do because they are terrified to let anyone actually know they might be less than perfect.

Insecurity is the feeling that you're never good enough to confront challenges and opportunities, makes you feel helpless in the face of problems, and tells you that you're incompetent to accomplish a particular task. You feel unaccepted, disapproved of, and rejected.

> » **MILLIONS OF PEOPLE SUFFER FROM INSECURITY, AND IT CAN BE A DEVASTATING FORCE THAT DIVERTS GOOD PEOPLE FROM THEIR POTENTIAL AND WREAKS HAVOC WITH FAMILIES, RELATIONSHIPS, ORGANIZATIONS, AND COMPANIES.**

Hollywood is rampant with insecurity. I worked with a television producer who was so insecure about being in charge, he refused to take any ideas or suggestions from anyone. He was terrified that if he took advice from someone, they would think he was an incompetent leader. The fact is, one of the characteristics of great leadership is taking advice and counsel from a number of sources.

Had he listened to the writers, directors, and others who surrounded him, he would have been highly successful, but he preferred to isolate himself and eventually went out of business. His insecurity drove him to become exactly what he feared the most—incompetent.

Insecurity is what keeps people from admitting mistakes because they're horrified that someone might think they're unintelligent. Some even go to huge lengths to cover or hide errors, to the extent that I believe the beginnings of many corporate scandals has been driven by insecurity and fear.

> » **THE PARADOX OF INSECURITY IS THAT IT DRIVES PEOPLE TO THE VERY PLACES, SITUATIONS, AND EMOTIONS THEY ARE DESPERATELY TRYING TO AVOID AT ALL COSTS.**

I urge you to take a serious look at your own life. Truly insecure people are often the most difficult to reach because they are so desperate to cover up what they feel are inadequacies and failures. No one is looking, and the only person who will benefit from this is you. Take a moment and consider if you have insecurities in your life.

As with many other issues in this book, I urge people who struggle with serious insecurities to find professional help through counselors, doctors, or pastors. But for most, here are some immediate suggestions that can help you begin to overcome insecurity and start the journey toward confidence and change.

OVERCOMING INSECURITY

Be willing to take a risk.

Yes, you might be hurt or embarrassed, but so what? To overcome insecurity and gain confidence, you need to allow yourself the freedom to take a chance. Realize that your behavior is alienating your closest friends and damaging your relationships and career. Start writing that book you've always dreamed about. Take music lessons. Speak at a conference. Buy that dress. Host a party. Take a risk, because a risk often comes with great rewards.

Jolt!

Learn to laugh at yourself.

Insecure people are so *serious* all the time. Lighten up and develop healthier attitudes. Stop your obsessive need for approval and acceptance, and learn to laugh at your mistakes. We're all human, and it's time to stop taking yourself so seriously. When you do make a mistake, be the first to make fun of yourself. You'll often find people are far more supportive than you think.

Start thinking realistically.

The best way to stand up to your fears and doubts is by approaching life from a more rational and realistic perspective. You aren't the center of the world here, and your little mistakes just don't mean much in the bigger picture. Besides, as you'll learn later in the chapter on failure, mistakes can be a much better teacher than success, so enroll in the class of life and start screwing up!

Reward yourself for the little victories.

When you finish your workout routine, reward yourself. When you successfully complete that big project, reward yourself. When you can take good advice or correction without feeling angry, reward yourself.

Jolt your security blanket and realize it's not about you. The very people you lash out at and hurt may be the same ones who are trying to help you the most. You are valuable, talented, skilled, and your worth is immeasurable. Stop looking at yourself through broken glasses and see yourself with 20/20 vision.

When you can do that, your insecurity will be replaced by a vibrant confidence in yourself and in your future.

REVIEW
Jolt Your Potential

List areas where you can begin to personally grow, then answer the following questions.

1. How can I begin? (Examples: purchase a teaching series, books, magazines, classes, etc.)
2. In what areas can I be more creative?
3. What aspects of my career need more creativity?
4. What areas of my life and career just don't make sense? Can I embrace that ambiguity and move forward?
5. Where can I give? (List charities, church ministries, social or community causes, humanitarian outreaches, and other areas where you can give your time, your money, and your expertise.)

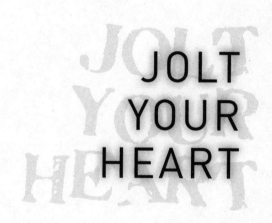

JOLT YOUR HEART

BUILD A MOTIVATION MACHINE

Personal Cheerleaders Can Make a Powerful Difference

I always wanted to be somebody. If I made it, it's half because I was game enough to take a lot of punishment along the way and half because there were a lot of people who cared enough to help me.

—ALTHEA GIBSON, AFRICAN-AMERICAN TENNIS CHAMPION

A friend is someone who will help you move.
A real friend is someone who will help you move a body.

—AUTHOR UNKNOWN

A disrupted world has revealed a tidal wave of critics. The rise of instant information has resulted in an overflow of nasty web-sites, celebrity tell-all blogs, and corporate whistle-blowers. On April 16, 2009, the national news broke the story that Domino's Pizza was taking a serious public relations hit after some of its employees posted videos of themselves on YouTube doing some pretty disgusting things in the kitchen of a Domino's restaurant in Conover, North Carolina.

Actually, I saw the videos, and "pretty disgusting" might be an understatement.

In the traditional business world before the digital age, the response would usually be "No response." In those days, companies could wait out the storm and ignore the small blip of bad PR, even if it had been picked up by the evening news. Containment usually meant "ignore it and it will go away." But in the online 24/7 connected world of text messaging, e-mail, Twitter, and Facebook, where bad news travels instantly and online videos can reach millions overnight, "No response" is the worst response of all.

Within hours, Patrick Doyle, president of Ann Arbor–based Domino's USA, in a two-minute YouTube video *produced by the company*, apologized to customers for the incident involving the two workers in North Carolina. Doyle said the company would be reviewing its hiring practices and that particular Domino's facility "has been shut down and sanitized from top to bottom."

BAD NEWS TRAVELS FAST ON THE WEB

Through various blogs and YouTube, the offending employee videos had been viewed by millions of people, and the situation was rapidly becoming a powerful yet tragic example of how social media can potentially tarnish a longtime brand virtually overnight. Immediate polling indicated the company's brand equity was dropping quickly. They were simply on the wrong end of a digital storm—a spontaneously formed online mob who rapidly shared information.

But Doyle's remarkably quick response to the employees and customer base was praised by numerous experts and observers—particularly his decision to use virtually the same websites and media that spread the offending video in the first place. While the company didn't emerge completely unscathed, it was a contemporary example of understanding the influence of the Internet in containing a potential public relations nightmare—what some are calling "social media terrorism." The truth is, the digital universe is hard to control, which is a significant reason many traditional brick-and-mortar companies have been so slow to go online.

While bad things happen online and every company needs to invest in protection, the world has shifted, and there's no going back.

THE POWER OF RUMOR

One of the fascinating and frustrating issues with the Web is the power of rumor. People are people and very often are willing to believe anything they

Take some time and think long and hard about your relationships. Starting today, spend more time cultivating and developing relationships with people who really care about you and your future. People who don't feel threatened by your success and who genuinely want to see you succeed.

You don't have to be cold or rude to the others. Maintain their friendships, but spend your serious time with those who believe in you and want you to achieve your potential.

True friends are those who really know you but love you anyway.
—EDNA BUCHANAN, PULITZER PRIZE WINNER

I go back to the saying, go where you are celebrated, not just tolerated. Good advice. The more time you spend with your personal cheerleaders, the more you'll stay motivated and energized. Who you listen to matters, so you need to surround yourself with people who fill you with emotional support.

I also suggest you assemble a small group of encouraging people and meet regularly with them to share ideas and dreams. The writers C. S. Lewis and J. R. R. Tolkien were members of a group associated with Oxford University, called the Inklings. It was a group of teachers, writers, and friends who met regularly at a well-known Oxford pub to discuss passages from their favorite books as well as their own writing. They shared the same moral and cultural values, religious beliefs, and education.

One of their chief concerns and regular points of discussion was the declining influence of faith within the culture. In 1936, they decided that the world needed novels that used issues of faith and morality as their central themes. Lewis and Tolkien decided to write science fiction, after realizing the poor level of similar stories being published at the time. They literally tossed a coin to decide who would write a book on space travel versus time travel. Tolkien got the time travel nod, but his early efforts with a story never really worked out. Later, however, he would achieve great success with *The Lord of the Rings*. Lewis wrote his famous series of novels called The Space Trilogy, and from that momentum he eventually penned The Chronicles of Narnia.

Meeting regularly with good friends is an invaluable source of encouragement and motivation—especially when those friends share your business interests, passion, and expertise.

*Call it a clan, call it a network, call it a tribe, call it a family. Whatever
you call it, whoever you are, you need one.*
—JANE HOWARD, NOVELIST

Another reason for cheerleaders is that one person can only carry a burden so far by himself. In the fifties, a young writer named John Kennedy Toole worked alone, writing a novel in New Orleans. He wasn't a particularly outgoing young man, and he carried the weight of writing and selling the manuscript totally on his own shoulders. When it was finished, he sent it to publisher after publisher, but few even responded. One major publisher initially liked it but ultimately rejected it. With no one to share his frustration, he was finally overcome by rejection, and when he could take it no more, he took his own life.

Sometime after the funeral, his mother found the coffee-stained manuscript, took up the cause, and became his champion. She finally found an LSU professor and accomplished writer named Walker Percy, who agreed to read it. She sent him the well-worn pages. When Percy read the story, he immediately recognized its genius and recommended it to a major publisher. After its release, John Kennedy Toole's novel, *A Confederacy of Dunces*, won a Pulitzer Prize and has been heralded as one of the major novels of the twentieth century.

I often wonder how things might have been different if that young writer had been surrounded by a group of intimate friends with whom he could have shared his burdens and who would have given him encouragement and love. People who could have helped him through the rejection letters from publishers, the challenges of writing, or the times when he struggled to fill the page.

*Keep away from people who try to belittle your ambitions. Small people always
do that, but the really great make you feel that you, too, can become great.*
—MARK TWAIN, WRITER AND HUMORIST

Your list of friends could probably use a jolt. Seek out the people who really believe in your potential. Encourage and support them, and welcome their support in return. Spend time with people who energize you, challenge you, and make you better, and cut down on your time with those who drain your energy, time, and talent.

Friends who will speak positive words of encouragement into your life are more valuable than gold. Treat them with the same care and respect.

THE FREEDOM OF ACCOUNTABILITY

The Secret of *Real* Independence

Liberty means responsibility. That is why most men dread it.
—GEORGE BERNARD SHAW, PLAYWRIGHT

The price of greatness is responsibility.
—SIR WINSTON CHURCHILL, BRITISH PRIME MINISTER

Earlier I told the story of a man who spent years wrestling with pornography. I return to that story because it's an example of a problem that is remarkably difficult to correct. Although most researchers would not consider pornography a classic disease, it can be a legitimate addiction. For instance, researchers have documented the dramatic role pornography plays for career criminals and how it can actually consume their lives. In addition, as with a drug, the porn addict is in constant need of an ever-growing "fix." What seemed like a fun experience looking at simple pinup shots suddenly demands that he look at more explicit photos, until even hard-core pornography isn't enough to satisfy his increased desire.

One man who went through that nightmare and was able to emerge on the other side is a pastor from the Midwest. I met Mike when I did some consulting at a large church where he was working on staff. I could tell he was far more experienced than a typical assistant and asked him numerous times if he had been a senior pastor before. Finally, after a long meeting, he asked if I could join him for dinner, where he told me his remarkable story.

Years before, as a young pastor, Mike was making a small salary and couldn't afford much when it came to shopping for a home. He and his wife finally bought a condo in a less desirable part of town. One morning, while taking out the trash, he found a paperback book sitting next to the dumpster. Not thinking much of it, he flipped it open to discover it was a hard-core pornographic novel. He only needed to read a few lines to see this wasn't something for him, so he quickly dropped the paperback into the bag and continued dumping the trash.

But days later, a strange thing happened. Those few lines from the novel he thought he had forgotten came back to his mind. Even then, he didn't think much of it and quickly thought about something else.

But the thoughts continued. Days and weeks later, he just couldn't get those few graphic and explicit lines from the pornographic novel out of his mind. It was like a worm that had dug its way into his brain and just wouldn't leave.

Within a few months he began to be obsessed with the thoughts and wanted more. He tried to forget about it, but it just latched on and wouldn't let go. Then one day he left the church office early, stopped by a newsstand on the way home, and picked up an adult magazine. The desire was being fed. It wasn't long before his wife went on a weekend church mission trip and he decided to rent an adult video. One thing led to another, and within a year he was traveling to nearby towns to visit adult bookstores. Eventually he gained the courage to visit a "massage parlor."

The successful young pastor was completely out of control, and his addiction to pornography was escalating. His habit was costing him upward of one thousand dollars a month, and he became very skillful at not letting his wife see the credit card bills. In addition, he was isolating himself from the very people who could have helped—his wife, his family, and other pastors. Over and over he tried to stop, but the pull was just too strong.

Finally, he realized it had to end, but the only way out he could think of was suicide. One night he purchased a handgun and decided this would be his last night on the earth. But in the darkness, he somehow found the courage to put down the gun and confess to his wife.

Needless to say, the confession was a shock. She still loved him and believed in him, but after his explicit description of the lie he had lived during the last two years, she appropriately decided to draw new boundaries on their relationship. He slept in the guest room, and they decided to seek counseling from a trusted and qualified pastor.

The professional counseling process, getting his spiritual and moral priorities back in order, and Mike's slow but determined decision to overcome his addiction and get his life back on track is a remarkable story.

That night over dinner when Mike told me the story of his recovery, the one thing that stood out on his journey back to health and wholeness was accountability. The first thing Mike did was to leave the ministry in order to take the time to work through the problem. The second thing he did was to set up a relationship of accountability with another pastor. He said that without the element of accountability, all the counseling, education, and love in the world would have failed.

> » **ACCOUNTABILITY IS CRITICAL IN A DIGITAL CULTURE WHERE INDISCRETIONS ARE NEARLY IMPOSSIBLE TO HIDE.**

Accountability is simply agreeing with a trusted friend who will hold you to your promises—someone you meet with regularly, who knows you intimately, who isn't afraid to speak the truth in love, who will call you to excellence, and who will force you to stay the course. When I met Mike, it was after two years of accountability and counseling. His marriage was stronger than ever, and he had grown to the point that another pastor had given him the chance to be mentored under his leadership, as the first step of his eventual restoration into full-time ministry.

The changes you need to make may not have anything to do with an addiction to pornography. (Although for male readers, I would urge you to do a gut check on your desires and feelings in this area. Most of us guys love to see a beautiful woman, and in a society where sexuality is flaunted, it's often difficult to avoid taking that second look. So it never hurts to understand that, for most males, the potential for sexual blunders is significant, and I would suggest you not only stay on the alert but also keep an ongoing dialogue with your wife or friend about the issue.)

But even if the immediate changes you need to make are in other areas, accountability is still critical. Find someone you know, trust, and respect. (I say this because if it's someone you don't respect, chances are, you won't take his warnings or advice.) Share with him your desire for change, and both of you agree that you'll work together to help keep you on the path toward real change.

TIPS ON ACCOUNTABILITY

Find the right person.

It might be your doctor, pastor, spouse, mentor, or a respected friend. In most cases, I don't recommend someone from the office since the political pressures of the workplace might come into play. You need to find a person who isn't intimidated by you and who will tell you the truth in love, no matter what. Finding someone who knows something about the particular area you're trying to change is good. For instance, if you want to improve your leadership skills, your spouse might not be the best accountability partner. On the other hand, if you want to improve your listening, he or she might be perfect.

Find someone with your personal values. For instance, if spiritual faith is important to you, don't pick someone who trivializes religion; or if you're a political conservative, pick another political conservative. The same holds true for a liberal. The point is, you don't want your time together derailed because of conflicting beliefs or values, so find a partner who shares your personal views on morality, ethics, values, and even political ideals. The purpose of these sessions is accountability, not debate, so you don't want to waste your precious time arguing about issues that have nothing to do with your desire for change.

Meet together on a regular basis.

Generally, I recommend once or twice a month. If it's a critical change, however, you might want to meet on a weekly basis. Share your progress, ask for insights and suggestions, and be completely open and transparent. No one can help you if you're holding back, so if you want real change, spill your guts.

If you want to change your attitude toward people, tell your accountability partner if you've been short with an assistant or rude to another employee. If you want to change your time management skills, tell him how many times you were late this week. Your accountability partner can't help you if you hold back, so give him the information he needs so he can help you progress.

Probably the best accountability partner is another person who wants to grow and change. I suggest you find someone who wants to change in other areas, but the fact that your partner also wants to change will make him or her more committed and helpful in your situation. Plus, it's always encouraging when you can help that individual as well, because it gives you both an increased motivation to grow.

Consider more than one accountability partner.

I know many executives who meet with a group of two or three people. Too many becomes time-consuming and unwieldy, but multiple members of a group can often bring more insight and wisdom to the mix.

> » A REAL ACCOUNTABILITY PARTNER IS A "TEAM MEMBER" WHO'S DEDICATED TO YOUR SUCCESS. PICK YOUR PARTNERS WISELY, MEET WITH THEM REGULARLY, AND COMMIT TO THE PROCESS.

How long should the relationship last? Technically, it should last until you've experienced genuine change. But the fact is, I know many people who started holding each other accountable in a particular area and have continued meeting for years, long after the initial purpose was accomplished. Even after they overcame their initial challenge, they found that meeting with a trusted friend on a regular basis to share experiences, obstacles, and frustrations is a fantastic tool for personal growth.

Something important to mention is that outside of a husband/wife relationship, accountability partners should be of the same gender. Intimate details and challenges are often discussed in these meetings, and it's simply not healthy for a man and woman to share this type of information—especially if either person is married to someone else. Integrity plays an important role here, and you'll achieve far better results if issues of gender and sexuality don't play a role.

Also, when you meet, it's important to realize the confidential nature of the sessions. This isn't professional counseling, but it's critical that each of you is comfortable that what you say will not be passed on to others.

Finally, understand the critical importance of "confession." If you don't share the honest reality of what you've been experiencing, then the fact that you meet on a regular basis won't do you much good. In this case, confession isn't a religious act, but it is confessing your mistakes, shortcomings, and errors and getting them off your chest. But for confession to work, it has to be real, heartfelt, and sincere. The old adage that confession is good for the soul is correct. The Bible calls it *sin*, and although that word has fallen out of fashion today, it still is the best term I can think of for willful disobedience, cheating, lying, stealing, or compromising our integrity.

» **PRESIDENT BILL CLINTON'S PHRASE HAS NOW BECOME IMMORTAL:"I DID NOT HAVE SEXUAL RELATIONS WITH THAT WOMAN."**

When we do make those mistakes, there's something about confession that begins the healing process. Acknowledging our mistakes and sincerely asking for forgiveness will open a door.

In a spiritual sense, God knows we made the mistake, but getting it out in the open is a major step to wholeness.

In her book *The Power of a Praying Woman*, Stormie Omartian said:

> Confessing, however, is more than just apologizing. Anyone can do that. We all know people who are good apologizers. The reason they are so good at it is because they get so much practice. They have to say "I'm sorry" over and over again because they never change their ways. In fact, they sometimes say, "I'm sorry" without ever actually admitting any fault. Those are the professional apologizers. And their confessions don't mean anything. But *true* confession means admitting in full detail what you have done and then fully repenting of it. (39–40)

Historically, *repentance* has meant "changing your mind." It's the idea that you realize your mistakes, confess them openly, and make an honest, heartfelt decision to change. But the fact is, it's a rare event in the lives of most people.

I worry sometimes what that teaches our children. Today we live in a society where an entire generation is very familiar with avoiding responsibility. It's much easier to pass the buck and blame someone else. We cheat, lie, and steal, but it's really someone else's fault.

Accountability is the key to changing the direction of our culture. When you accept the responsibility for what you need to change, when you partner with someone who sincerely wants to help you change, and when you commit to making the change, then real results begin to happen.

Find an accountability partner today and begin the process.

THE POWER OF PERCEPTION

Why It Is Just as Important as Reality

Science is nothing but perception.

—PLATO

Ransom Stoddard: You're not going to use the story, Mr. Scott?
Maxwell Scott: No, sir. This is the West, sir. When the legend
becomes fact, print the legend.

—THE MAN WHO SHOT LIBERTY VALANCE

Earlier I talked about filming at the headwaters of the Amazon River basin in Brazil. What I didn't mention was the trouble we ran into when we attempted to get our film equipment through customs in the Brazilian city of Manaus. The city is located about one thousand miles upriver from the Atlantic and today is a beautiful city of nearly two million people. When we arrived at the airport, which had been literally carved out of the jungle, I had a three-man crew and a number of large cases of film equipment that had to be cleared through customs.

"Can you prove you're a filmmaker from the United States?"

I had my passport, customs documentation, and equipment lists, but I'd never actually been asked to prove what I do for a living. After all, it's not like we carry a membership card or diploma around to prove we're in some type of "filmmaker's club."

"Well I'm sorry, Mr. Cooke. Until you can prove to me you're actually an official filmmaker from the United States, I can't allow your equipment into the country. You're welcome to come in, but I'll have to keep your equipment locked here in customs until you can provide adequate documentation."

Official filmmaker? It was insane. It's not like tourists carry nearly a million dollars' worth of film and video equipment on vacation. We argued and argued, but nothing worked. So I took the crew to the hotel, frustrated and upset because we still had airplane flights, boat charters, and numerous other connections to meet, and now everything was being thrown into chaos. We paced the hotel room, thinking, tried to make phone calls, and discussed every possible solution but came up empty.

The jungle heat and humidity didn't help. Every day we would travel back to the customs official and request the equipment, and every day he would turn us down. Assuming he was corrupt, we even quietly offered him a bribe since that technique had worked in similar situations, but no dice—he was an honest guy, but he just wouldn't budge.

After a few days, we considered returning to the United States in failure, knowing we had wasted thousands of dollars to get this far, with nothing to show for it.

The problem was *perception*. No matter how many passports, equipment lists, and travel arrangements I showed the customs official, for some reason he was convinced we weren't actual filmmakers. We argued until we were exhausted, but his *perception* just wouldn't change.

Finally, after four days of haggling and arguing with no success, I walked slowly back to my room, annoyed, knowing we had tried everything and still failed. Getting ready to undress for the night, I pulled my wallet out of my jeans pocket and for some unknown reason decided to flip through the back section, where I kept my insurance cards and driver's license, and that's when the card that changed everything fell out.

Years before, a nonprofit organization in Hollywood began publishing *American Film*, a magazine devoted to filmmaking. It was a wonderful magazine for anyone who truly loved movies, because it wasn't just another trendy publication about movie stars. It featured real articles about the behind-the-scenes process of making films, intimate interviews, interesting stories, and other information about the industry. The magazine was a highly respected division of an organization still in existence today called the American Film

Institute, which conducts classes and workshops for serious filmmakers and even sponsors major industry events.

At that time, when you signed up for a subscription to the magazine, you received a membership card into the American Film Institute. It didn't really mean anything more than the magazine subscription, except that it might get you into an occasional film screening.

When the American Film Institute magazine subscription card fell out of my wallet, I had a brilliant idea, and the next morning we were back in the customs official's office.

"You want proof that we are filmmakers from the United States, right?"

"That's correct, and so far, I've seen nothing."

I whipped out my AFI card—fortunately, the information on the card about the magazine subscription was printed on the back in very small letters, and I hoped he wouldn't notice.

"I'm a member of the American Film Institute." I pointed at the front. "There, you can see my name printed on my membership card."

The customs official looked at the card carefully, compared the signature with my passport, and then a light switched on in his head.

"Why didn't you tell me you were a member of the American Film Institute?" He beamed with excitement, as if he'd stumbled on a real celebrity. He had no idea what the AFI was, but it sure sounded impressive.

"Welcome to our country! Please enjoy your filming!"

He walked around the desk, embraced everyone on my crew, and then led us into the warehouse where they were holding our equipment. He couldn't have been nicer. The next thing we knew, we were being given a police escort with full sirens and lights back to the hotel, with government trucks personally carrying our equipment and personnel unloading it for us.

> » **THE INFLUENCE OF THE MASS MEDIA IN OUR CULTURE IS CHANGING EVERYTHING, AND "PERCEPTION" IS THE LANGUAGE SPOKEN BY MODERN MEDIA.**

I kissed my AFI membership card, carefully tucked it away in my wallet, and carried it carefully for years—even after the actual magazine ceased publication. The simple magazine subscription card meant nothing in itself, but it changed the perception of that customs official completely. When his perception changed, we went from being tourists at best—con artists at worst—to being celebrated filmmakers from the United States, deserving official government approval and support.

In more than thirty years of active work in the entertainment industry, I've seen few situations where perception played such an important role.

In a world where sound bites heavily influence the political process, the unique characteristics of mass media now affect every aspect of our lives. Public relations has become an art form as companies and organizations (and even celebrities) confront the need to impact and hopefully influence public opinion, and perception has become a critical part of advertising campaigns, press releases, and public statements.

The global fascination with celebrities has been an important element in the realization of how important perception is today. For instance, with the advent of the relatively recent concept of "celebrity," the basis of fame has undergone a striking change. In the past, a person became famous for accomplishing a significant task, such as making a great discovery, winning the championship football game, or finding the cure for a deadly disease. But today, just being in the news makes someone famous, and actual accomplishment really isn't necessary anymore. A movie star showing up at a party makes front-page news, high-profile sexual affairs propel some to national TV interviews and book deals, and paparazzi photographers have made "celebrity journalism" the foundation of entire magazines.

There's an interesting aspect to why the advertising industry has moved from "informational" advertising to "emotional" advertising. Since the beginning of modern advertising, the primary goal of marketers was to tell the public about the wonderful features of a product—how it works, the quality of the construction, or the helpful features. But today, advertisers don't tell us *about the product*, they tell us *how we're going to feel when we use the product*. When was the last time you saw an athletic shoe commercial that described the high-quality materials that went into the shoes, the excellent construction, or the useful features? Today they're more interested in convincing you that when you strap on these shoes, you'll suddenly leap like an all-star, win championship sports events, or fit in with a cooler crowd.

It's that way in nearly every product area. It's not about facts anymore; it's about perception. In my book *Branding Faith: Why Some Churches and Nonprofits Impact Culture and Others Don't*, I discuss the power of perception and its impact on nonprofit and religious work around the world.

» HOLLYWOOD SPENDS MILLIONS TO CONTROL PERCEPTIONS.

Since the earliest days of the movie industry, the major studios have created vast machines to control the perception of movie stars and the movies they produced. In fact, back in those days it was not unusual for major studios to have local government officials, members of the press, or police officers on a secret payroll so they could quietly control the impact of potentially high-profile scandals. If movie stars featured in family-friendly movies were caught committing adultery, being drunk and disorderly, or in a criminal act, the studios could call in favors from elected officials or the press to keep a lid on the news.

Public morals and behavior have changed so much that it almost seems as if the studios must encourage rowdy behavior, but you can be sure that whatever image they want to create for a particular star is still carefully guarded and controlled—even if the questionable methods of an older era have been largely relinquished. In fact, the entertainment industry has given rise to the professional "publicist"—someone whose job it is to help direct and control the perception of a movie, a TV series, or a star.

Outside of Hollywood the art of perception is used every day to promote positive projects, people, values, or ideas. For instance, major business leaders are getting into the picture and hiring publicists because they've discovered that controlling perception not only works with companies and products, it also works with people. In today's environment of celebrity, CEOs around the country know that being seen in the right places can help them meet the right people, be perceived as major players, and open doors for new strategic opportunities.

» PERCEPTION IS A POWERFUL WORD AND HAS ENORMOUS CONSEQUENCES.

But how can we use perception in our own lives? To what extent can we influence the way others perceive us, and how can we use those techniques to make change happen and accomplish our goals?

First, understand that perception can be a positive tool. Too many people view the perception issue as a negative tool of manipulation and refuse to consider its positive potential. They've seen the way some alcohol advertisers have attempted to influence teens to drink, or the way some cigarette companies tried to do the same with smoking, and assume any use of influence is negative. The fact is, many people in all levels of our society have misused the power of perception, and our culture suffers the consequences. The pornography industry uses perception to legitimize what they do, casinos never mention the high level of gambling-related suicides, and even street-level cocaine dealers use perception to make drug use attractive.

I've had the opportunity to teach around the world, and one of my favorite places to lecture is Russia, where I've taught media and broadcasting techniques in Moscow and St. Petersburg. When you study the history of communism in the former Soviet Union, you'll find that Lenin was a master of perception and used these techniques in a negative way to keep millions of people under the brutal hand of the Soviet state. Lenin always felt that cinema was the greatest art form, because he understood the power of movies to inspire, motivate, and educate. Under his control, the Russian film industry grew at an enormous rate but was used as a terrible tool to help subjugate the Russian people for decades.

In spite of its abuse, the power of perception can be utilized for good—if we know how to activate it in our lives.

Second, start thinking in reverse. It's not the message you send; it's the message that's received that counts. It doesn't matter how brilliant you are, if your intention is misunderstood by the listener, then you've failed miserably. That's why I always prefer to start at the receiving end first—just to make sure my message has the best chance of being received properly. How do I do it? I realize that every listener is evaluating my message through his or her own framework of life experiences, which dictate to a great extent the impact it will have on him or her personally. Therefore, know whom you're dealing with and know them as well as possible. Whatever your business, make sure you tailor your product, presentation, or service to a particular audience.

I always tailor my lectures to the audience. Sometimes I speak to corporations, other times I speak to nonprofit or religious groups, and still other times to college students. In each situation I may deliver the same information, but I consider the audience first and customize the message to reach that audience most effectively.

Don't begin with your message, begin with the audience.

THE IMPORTANCE OF PACKAGING

When I was a kid, television meant three channels. Whoopee! But on our satellite TV system today, children have a choice of five hundred channels, and online that number is nearly unlimited. The difference is extraordinary and very important.

My production experience in a five-hundred-channel universe indicates that people take fewer than five seconds to decide to watch your program. That's it. Think about how quickly you handle a typical TV remote and what little chance you give each program to grab your attention. Audiences today are sophisticated and aren't willing to put up with programs that don't interest them. Therefore I always advise my media clients that how a program is packaged is just as important as its content. For instance, no matter how brilliant the program content might be, it has to be packaged in a high-quality, contemporary, and compelling way. Otherwise the viewer won't watch long enough to hear the content, and you've lost the audience.

In the same way, you need a compelling "package" in order to be perceived as powerfully as possible. What elements combine to make your package great? Here are a few to consider.

How You Look

Clothes make the man. Naked people have little or no influence on society.
—MARK TWAIN

My father used to say, "If you dress like a pauper, you'll never get an audience with the king." Although styles today are much more relaxed than in the past, there are still strong feelings among people about clothes and the impact they have on perception. Even in Hollywood, where jeans are considered "business attire," if you look closely, you'll find those jeans are often accompanied by an exotic leather belt, an expensive linen sport coat, a designer T-shirt, a pair of alligator loafers, and a twenty-thousand-dollar watch.

But understand that it's not about money; it's about a style that's appropriate for the situation. Don't become a clothing snob and use clothes as a weapon to elevate yourself above others. No one respects a person in the office who uses clothes as a label to separate from everyone else. But do know and learn the power of how to dress appropriately and how clothes can be used to give you access to people, places, and events.

How You Speak

Make sure you have finished speaking before your audience
has finished listening.
—DOROTHY SARNOFF, OPERA SINGER

At the highest levels of corporate America, you rarely hear the sound of regional accents. A Southern accent sprinkled with local mannerisms may sound cute in your hometown, but the more you travel beyond the city limits, the more you'll sound simply out of place. Talking like a cast member of *The Sopranos* may be desirable in parts of New Jersey, but in parts of Texas you could be shot on sight.

Proper grammar is another basic issue that frightfully few take the time to fix. If you want to increase your value and perception in the eyes of other people, never open your mouth unless you're speaking standard English and using grammatically correct sentences. Remember that, in most business situations, your speaking voice and writing abilities are your most important communication tools; therefore, poor grammar muddles up your meaning.

No matter how old you are, it's never too late to improve your communication abilities. A quarterback wouldn't neglect his passing skills, because that's often the key to his success. In the same way, your brilliance and business expertise will never be known or understood if you can't express those ideas clearly and accurately.

Appropriate Behavior

Those that are good manners at the court are as ridiculous in the country,
as the behavior of the country is most mockable at the court.
—WILLIAM SHAKESPEARE

Knowing instinctively how to act in a variety of situations is a critical element to improving perception. Some football coaches are brilliant on the field, but at a dinner party they become bumbling fools. In the same way, I've met doctors who are internationally known for their medical skills in the operating room but act ignorant and uncouth in other situations. Learn to become comfortable in a wide variety of circumstances, and your chances of success are greatly improved.

At a board meeting, a formal dinner party, a local football game, or church, in a casual social situation or on a business trip, does your behavior reflect the level of success you're working toward? And please don't think the value of perception is the ability to hide the fact that, in reality, you are unethical or dishonest. Ethical and moral behavior matters. It creates trust, loyalty, and integrity, and when damaged, reputations are tough and often impossible to rebuild.

Everything communicates.
—BRAD ABARE, BRANDING AND ORGANIZATIONAL CONSULTANT

Start today recognizing opportunities to jolt your perception in the eyes of your superiors, your customers, and your associates. A business genius who neglects the value of perception risks appearing to others as simply average, or worse, a fool. On the other hand, even a relative novice in business and leadership skills can dramatically improve his standing among his associates through an investment in the art of perception.

Who you are is important, and so is the impact of how you are perceived.

CHANGE YOUR THINKING AND CHANGE YOUR FUTURE

The Incredible Influence of Your Thought Life

*The significant problems we have cannot be solved
at the same level of thinking with which we created them.*

—ALBERT EINSTEIN, PHYSICIST

Elevate your thinking, and you elevate your life.

—KEITH CRAFT, LEADERSHIPOLOGY.COM

*R*eal positive thinking isn't empty platitudes or "wishful" dreaming. It's not a shallow attempt at getting employees motivated to do their best, or something only stupid people follow. Yes, that type of positive thinking is out there. You most often see it on posters with beautiful landscapes with cute little quotes in the corner, or engraved on plaques hanging on the wall of office cubicles.

*A motivational speaker makes you feel good,
but the next day you don't know why.*

—JOHN MAXWELL, LEADERSHIP EXPERT, AUTHOR, AND SPEAKER

Shallow attempts at "positive thinking" drive me nuts. But when you get past that surface level of motivation (or pseudomotivation), you discover that *real* positive thinking affects the core of your being. How you think determines your outlook, your attitude, your persistence, and your approach. It changes your perspective on life and therefore can literally change the outcome of your situation.

Thinking determines action. In fact, one of the most fascinating elements of the teachings of Jesus Christ is the link between thought and action. When Jesus taught two thousand years ago, one of his greatest challenges was from religious leaders who acted piously on the outside but were dark and evil on the inside. He taught that you don't just commit a sin by actually physically doing the act, but you can also commit the sin just by *thinking* about it: "You have heard that it was said to those of old, 'You shall not commit adultery.' But I say to you that whoever looks at a woman to lust for her has already committed adultery with her in his heart" (Matthew 5:27–28 NKJV).

Was Jesus some type of cosmic killjoy who wanted to ruin our appreciation of beautiful women? Didn't he understand that it's a natural thing for men to look?

Actually, more than any person in history, Jesus understood life and how we live it. Remember, he turned water into wine at a marriage feast to save the day—so he certainly wasn't a prude. But Jesus understood the power of our minds. He knew that what we think can easily turn into action, so he was simply warning us about the power of our thoughts and how they can either make us better or destroy us.

> *Whether you think you can or you think you can't, you're probably right.*
> —HENRY FORD

Obviously, our minds can't do the impossible. There have been false religious systems created on the idea that our thoughts can do anything, and that idea simply isn't realistic or possible.

Sadly, there are always people who are gullible and tend toward the extreme in just about anything. But aside from the fringe, the fact is that there is enormous power in the way we think and what we think about.

> *The important thing in science is not so much to obtain*
> *new facts as to discover new ways of thinking about them.*
> —SIR WILLIAM BRAGG, NOBEL PRIZE IN PHYSICS, 1915

I've discovered in my consulting work with organizations that my first great challenge is always to change people's thinking. We can change the company's direction, the mission statement, the vision, the priorities, and even change the budget. But we'll never get anywhere until we can change how the employees think.

It's not an easy task. We all think in ways that were shaped by our upbringing and circumstances. Our parents had an enormous influence on the way we think and what we value. My father loved books, and guess what? So do I. Reading is one of my greatest passions, and my idea of a perfect day is to be snowed in at a mountain cabin with a fire in the hearth and a stack of books next to my chair. That love of reading came directly from the influence of my dad.

Chances are, key elements of your thinking came from your mother or father. Another key to our thinking is the group of people who have influenced us during the course of our lives. Perhaps it was a great teacher, coach, or family friend. Our thinking habits weren't born in a vacuum but were planted, watered, and nurtured by our closest family members and friends.

But no thinking pattern is locked. We can always change our thinking to make us more productive, positive, successful, and fulfilled. Good thinking is not involuntary; it's something we control, and as a result, it's something we can change.

Few people think more than two or three times a year; I have made an international reputation for myself by thinking once or twice a week.
—GEORGE BERNARD SHAW, PLAYWRIGHT

CONSIDER FOR A MOMENT YOUR STYLE OF THINKING

Are you naturally positive?

Do you meet most challenges with a positive response? Is it tough to really get you down or depressed? Are you the most encouraging person in your company?

Are you naturally negative?

Yes, there are people who deal with life in a very negative way, and you might be one of those people. Do you face every challenge with responses like,

"Well, I told you so. Nothing ever works out for me"? Do you naturally *expect* projects to fail? There was an executive who to this day is the most negative person I have ever encountered. When you walked into her office, you felt a darkness in the room. She was insecure and incompetent and looked at everything from the most negative angle possible. She yelled at everyone, believed that nothing would ever work out, and was depressed most of the time. She was finally fired when her boss realized that everyone in the company would walk out if management didn't do something immediately. She was toxic, and her negative thinking affected everyone around her.

There is no question that she's an extreme example, but millions of people have a negative thinking style that hinders them from breaking through barriers and experiencing success.

Are you naturally critical?

I have a tendency to be critical, and I have to fight to overcome this deadly style of thinking. As a television and film director, I've spent years on a set, judging aspects of the production. Is the acting natural? Is the set design what it needs to be? Is the lighting the most appropriate? Evaluating and being critical is my job, but I have to be careful to leave it at work. Unleashed at home or in other situations, it can be deadly.

Are you naturally reflective?

Do you think before speaking? Do you hold your thoughts until enough information is in? Do you prefer to sit back and not commit? Are you naturally shy and bashful?

INCREASE YOUR POTENTIAL THROUGH BETTER THINKING

Avoid the crowd. Do your own thinking independently.
Be the chess player, not the chess piece.
—RALPH CHARELL, MOTIVATIONAL WRITER

Quality of thinking. It's a phrase we don't hear about much, but it's absolutely critical to changing your life. I'm always amazed watching the employee dynamics of an organization. When I assemble a creative team around a conference table and throw out a challenge, it's fascinating to see how different people respond. Some grasp the challenge immediately and take off running. Others prefer to think about it first, and still others blow it off, open their laptops, and start answering e-mail.

Everyone approaches a challenge differently.

The mind ought sometimes to be diverted that
it may return the better to thinking.
—PHAEDRUS (15 BC–AD 50)

Jack Welch, legendary former CEO of General Electric, said, "99.9 percent of all employees are in the pile because they don't think."

Rise up. Stand above the others. Get out of the pile. The key is the quality of your thinking.

How do you do it? Start thinking of your brain as a muscle and exercise it. Read, learn, challenge yourself, push the limits of your thinking. Perhaps more important than anything, set aside a time during the day when you do nothing but think.

Leadership expert John Maxwell has profoundly influenced me when it comes to thinking. John has actually set aside a chair in his office where he thinks. He doesn't use it for anything else—when he's in that chair, he just sits and thinks.

I encourage you to do the same. Don't take phone calls, go to meetings, answer e-mail, or update your Facebook page in that chair. That's your "thinking chair," and thinking is the only thing you use it for. Every day—probably near the end of your day—take some time and sit in the chair, with only a pad and pencil, and think. Reflect on the day, think about the future, jot down notes, and just think.

When you make thinking a priority in your life, the quality of your life will dramatically increase. It's almost as if your brain is flattered that you're making it a priority, because believe me, it will respond. When you take that important time to reflect and think—and make it a daily habit—you'll be amazed at how the quality of your ideas will increase (not to mention the quantity).

MAXIMIZE YOUR GIFTS AND SKILLS THROUGH STRATEGIC THINKING

Discovery consists of seeing what everybody
has seen and thinking what nobody has thought.
—ALBERT VON SZENT-GYORGYI, NOBEL PRIZE IN MEDICINE, 1937

When filmmaker George Lucas created the Star Wars series of films, he didn't set out to impact the greater culture. He didn't know he would be producing some of the highest-grossing films of all time and creating the movie merchandising phenomenon we take for granted today.

But he did know he wanted to maximize his gifts and talents through the filmmaking process. When you study the story of how Lucas created the movies, struggled for the financing, and dealt with the major film studios, you find that he was very strategic in his thinking. He wasn't about to give in on any point he didn't have to, and he focused his thinking on a strategy that would not only get the first film made but would also open a doorway for an entire series of movies. The fact is, his remarkable thinking changed much of the way movies are marketed and merchandised. His films have become cinematic history, largely because George Lucas was able to maximize his personal gifts, talents, and skills through strategic thinking.

Strategic thinking is all about purpose. "We'll see what happens . . ." is a certain indication of the absence of strategic thinking. Strategists never leave anything to chance. They observe and calculate each step in their progression to success.

MULTIPLY YOUR OPTIONS THROUGH CREATIVE THINKING

You sort of start thinking anything's possible if you've got enough nerve.
—J. K. ROWLING, *HARRY POTTER AND THE ORDER OF THE PHOENIX*

Creative thinking is all about options—about new and innovative ways of doing what most people think is routine.

The great painter Pablo Picasso said, "There are painters who transform the sun to a yellow spot, but there are others who with the help of their art and their intelligence transform a yellow spot into the sun."

Creative thinking opens doors that are closed to the vast majority of people because it allows you to see options they can't see.

Before anyone else, Fred Smith envisioned a company that would deliver packages anywhere in the United States overnight. Before anyone else, Thomas Edison saw cities lighted by electricity. They both were great businessmen, but they were also creative thinkers.

I learned an unusual example of creative thinking years ago at a birthday party for a friend in Los Angeles. While at the party, I met a businessman who told me a remarkable story. He was sitting in a shopping mall four years earlier and noticed all the teenagers talking on their cell phones. He starting thinking about the connections—teenagers, cell phones, popular music—and thought that they might really enjoy being able to download ringtones of popular songs to their cell phones. So he assembled a small team who designed a website that would allow people to select a song and, for a small charge, upload it from the website to their phone.

That was four years earlier—before anyone had ever heard of "ringtones."

He told me that he had recently sold the company to a major corporation for about $40 million.

How many of us have watched teenagers talking on cell phones and not thought a thing about it? But by using creative thinking and making some innovative connections, with very little money he created a company that sold for $40 million in just four years.

OVERCOME DEFEAT AND OBSTACLES
THROUGH *REAL* POSITIVE THINKING

The word impossible *is not in my dictionary.*
—GENERAL NAPOLEON BONAPARTE

As I said before, what I call *real* positive thinking is not shallow and trivial. It's not wishful or unrealistic. Authentic positive thinking is an accurate picture of the possibilities and what can be accomplished in a given situation.

Real positive thinking looks at obstacles most people call impossible and laughs. Not because we're being stupid but because we've done our homework, have confidence in our abilities and skill, appreciate the mysterious, and are unhindered by fear. Real positive thinking is how underdogs make a living. It's how battles are turned and championship teams are upset.

Positive thinking isn't denial; it's the accurate realization that we don't, in fact, know everything, and therefore, anything could be possible.

Normal Vincent Peale wrote, "Formulate and stamp indelibly on your mind a mental picture of yourself as succeeding. Hold this picture tenaciously. Never permit it to fade. Your mind will seek to develop the picture."

Religious tradition has taught the mind-body connection for thousands of years. Recent studies show that a mental attitude has a significant impact on the body's ability to heal, and doctors are now taking the mental attitude of their patients very seriously.

Talk to athletes or business leaders and you'll find a remarkable similarity in the way they think about "thinking." Mental attitude is a key for championship athletes, and it can be a key for you as well.

EXPERIENCE SUCCESS THROUGH LONG-RANGE THINKING

A blockbuster movie takes 5–10 years to produce. So it's not about knowing what's popular now. To be really successful, you have to be thinking about what will be popular 5–10 years in the future.
—RALPH WINTER, PRODUCER *(X-MEN, WOLVERINE)*

To make change happen in your personal life or in the life of your company, you have to see things from a higher vantage point. It's not that different from looking at your house from street level and then seeing it from the window of a plane. It's a different world up there, and it puts the size of the house into a different category.

Most executives and leaders get stuck in crisis mode. Problems and challenges are hitting them on a daily, perhaps hourly, basis, and planning is difficult when you can't see beyond the immediate disaster. In that environment, it doesn't take long to sink deeper and deeper into the abyss and finally throw your hands up in failure.

But long-range planning can be done. Here are some suggestions for pulling your thinking out of an immediate crisis and considering your challenges from a greater distance:

Learn as much as you can about the competition.

Not necessarily to beat them, as much as to learn from them. Most people spend their careers either hating or ignoring the competition. Either way, you lose. You must realize that your perceived enemy can be your greatest friend. Learn from your competitors—both the good and the bad. The key is keeping an open mind. Leave your prejudices about their business at the door and objectively study how they work. It will expand your thinking and enlarge your perspective.

Study the legends in your business.

Why waste your life hitting walls, making mistakes, and tripping over obstacles, when you could easily learn from others who have gone before? Isaac Newton, considered by many to be the father of modern science, said, "If I have seen further it is by standing on the shoulders of giants." Study the lives and accomplishments of those in business, sports, politics, the arts, and other areas that could benefit you. Head to the biography section of your favorite bookstore and start reading. Learn from their mistakes, so you can move ahead faster and with much less frustration.

Become active in organizations related to your business or passion.

Becoming active in trade organizations, business seminars, and workshop events gives you the unique opportunity to network and discover new methods, new perspectives, and new techniques. Find out what others are doing and use that for your benefit. It will enlarge your vision and widen your perspective.

Nothing will jolt your thinking faster than seeing how others do your job. And nothing will help you appreciate your situation better than seeing other failures!

Reading furnishes the mind only with materials of knowledge;
it is thinking that makes what we read ours.
—JOHN LOCKE, PHILOSOPHER

Jolt!

Jolt your thinking today. Make good thinking intentional and deliberate, and make it a priority.

Your thoughts impact your life in very physical, tangible ways, and nothing you can do will contribute to changing your life more than transforming your thinking.

DISCOVER THE POWER OF FAITH

The Awesome Power in Looking Beyond Yourself

The most beautiful thing we can experience is the mysterious. It is the source of all true art and science. He to whom this emotion is a stranger, who can no longer pause to wonder and stand rapt in awe, is as good as dead: his eyes are closed.

—ALBERT EINSTEIN

He has put eternity in their hearts.

—ECCLESIASTES 3:11 NKJV

The search for eternal answers is so embedded in our DNA that without addressing spirituality we would miss a significant part of understanding the power of change. There are many books that address emotional, physical, and intellectual needs, but our spiritual longings are just as critical to a fulfilled life. When it comes to the faith that's played such an integral part in the making of America, however, we're suddenly getting a case of amnesia.

As I write this chapter, it is Christmas, and a great controversy is brewing across America. It has been reported that our culture has become so uncomfortable with Christianity that shopkeepers, clerks, executives, and salespeople are being advised to say "Happy holidays" rather than "Merry Christmas." Some school systems—mostly unaware of the law—are forbidding their students to sing Christmas carols in their concerts, and some are even referring to the season as "winter holidays" instead of "Christmas holidays."

At least we're not quite as far down that road as France. Major newspapers reported recently that even chocolate candy featuring religious themes was now banned from schools.

I comment on these developments not because I want to push religion down anyone's throat. I'm always ready to share my own personal journey of faith, but only when people are ready to listen. I write this because I grow more and more amazed at America's awkwardness with religious faith.

Yes, we need to be sensitive to people of all faiths. There was a place in ancient Greece called Mars Hill. It was where philosophers, thinkers, religious leaders, and writers of the time went to discuss new ideas. In many ways, it was a "marketplace" of beliefs, attitudes, religious ideas, and thought. When the apostle Paul visited Mars Hill to share the news about Jesus Christ, he not only recognized their gods but also was able to knowledgeably discuss their traditions and beliefs. Then, when he began sharing his own spiritual experience, it was in a direct but sensitive way, and not only did the audience listen, but many asked him to come back again.

But today, while our culture preaches tolerance, there is almost a hostility toward spiritual concepts and ideas—particularly those expressed through what is generally considered "organized" religion. As a result, we now have a generation that has grown up without any knowledge of spiritual principles whatsoever.

I was shopping for a gift for my wife in a jewelry market in downtown Los Angeles, when I noticed a young couple looking at necklaces. As they viewed the glass case, I overheard them discussing the various designs—particularly of the cross necklaces. At one end were simple, modern cross designs, while at the other end of the cabinet, the designs became more complex and ended with a section of traditional crosses with the figure of Jesus hanging on the crosses.

As the couple looked down the row of necklaces, I noticed that the woman suddenly stopped and remarked to her boyfriend, "Wow, those are really beautiful cross necklaces!" Then she stopped in her tracks. "But wait a second. Who's that little guy on those crosses over there?"

The young couple apparently had absolutely no idea who the figure of Jesus was hanging on the cross necklace.

Until relatively recently, that scene would never have happened.

From the time William Tyndale translated the Bible into English in 1526, its impact on the West has been overwhelming—even to the point of the development of the English language as we know it today. Phrases like "the skin of my teeth," "the handwriting on the wall," "still small voice," "a thorn in the flesh," "the fat of the land," "a law unto himself," and "root of all evil" are all common phrases taken directly from Tyndale's translation of the Bible. The Bible transformed literacy and learning even in the New World, as the first written form of many Native American languages was a result of the Bible being translated into their tongue. I recently saw an original Mohawk Bible on display in the Huntington Library in Los Angeles that was the first written record of that tribe's language.

The Bible's impact on literature has been even more significant. Without an understanding of the Bible, it would be difficult, if not impossible, to probe the depths of writers from Milton to Shakespeare.

But it doesn't stop there. The Bible has impacted novels from *Moby Dick* to *Uncle Tom's Cabin*, the development of Negro spirituals and gospel music, and the speeches of Abraham Lincoln. The fact is, you would have little understanding of Dr. Martin Luther King Jr.'s "I have a dream" speech without an understanding of the Bible. Whatever faith tradition you come from—or if you come from no faith perspective at all—I would encourage you to explore the spiritual aspect of your life.

» **WE ARE SPIRITUAL CREATURES, AND THROUGHOUT OUR LONG HISTORY, MANKIND HAS CONTINUALLY SEARCHED FOR ANSWERS TO THE QUESTIONS, WHY AM I HERE? WHAT IS MY PURPOSE? WHERE DID I COME FROM, AND WHERE AM I GOING?**

Playwright Eugène Ionesco wrote in his memoir:

In the history of humanity there are no civilizations or cultures which fail to manifest, in one or a thousand ways, this need for an absolute that is called heaven, freedom, a miracle, a lost paradise to be regained, peace, the going beyond history . . . there is no religion in which everyday life is not considered a prison; there is no philosophy or ideology that does not think that we live in alienation . . . Humanity has always had a nostalgia for the freedom that is only beauty, that is only real life, plenitude, light.

Since the Enlightenment began in the eighteenth century, Western Civilization has pursued the religion of science and reason. We have elevated scientific pursuit to the highest ideal, and we value scientific inquiry above all other pursuits. It has resulted in marvelous scientific progress, and much of the luxury we experience today has been the result of this relentless pursuit.

But at the beginning of the twenty-first century, after three hundred years of unbridled scientific pursuit, we still haven't answered the ultimate questions of our lives. Teen suicide continues in remarkable numbers, drugs and alcohol imprison millions, wars and genocide persist around the globe, families continue to fragment in ever-increasing numbers, cheating in school has reached record levels, happiness eludes us, and the quality of our lives is not significantly better.

For all of its wonderful advances, science has still been unable to answer eternal questions, such as:

Where did we come from?
Why are we here?
Do we have a purpose?
Where are we going?

In a development few would have predicted, some scientific advances are making us rethink the notion of a spiritual dimension to our lives. As more and more women are able to see their unborn children inside the womb through ultrasound technology, they are reconsidering the notion that a fetus is just a mass of cells.

On a trip to the United Kingdom, I noticed that London's *Sunday Times* in 2004 reported that Antony Flew, emeritus professor of philosophy at Reading University, whose writings and teachings on atheism have influenced an entire generation of thinkers and scholars around the world, had recanted his position and believes that some sort of deity *did* create the universe.

Flew died recently, and although far from becoming associated specifically with Christianity, he believed that, according to the Times, scientific discoveries have revealed the existence of an organizing intelligence. He went on to say that investigation of DNA "has shown, by the almost unbelievable complexity of the arrangements which are needed to produce life, that intelligence must have been involved."

An authentic spiritual journey is a journey of exploration, staying open to all detours, twists in the road, and new discoveries.

Do faith and reason conflict?

Absolutely not. The real man or woman of faith does not fear science, reason, or facts. And a scientist, confident in his or her abilities, has nothing to fear from spiritual inquiry.

The fact is, real faith can stand up to debate, inquiry, and investigation.

Writer C. S. Lewis came to his Christian faith only after years of investigation, study, and debate. He tried everything he could think of to discredit Christianity, and yet, in spite of his intellectual depth as a professor at Oxford, he could not find a single argument that disproved the reality of faith in God.

The key to living a vigorous life of faith is constant evaluation and investigation. Study, learn, discuss. Real faith is not a wishful hope in a vague concept. Real faith impacts the lives of everyone it touches.

Spiritual conviction was what drove the leaders of the civil rights movement to disregard police dogs, fire hoses, and jail for a cause they believed was true. Real faith is what fuels the persecuted church in countries where public expressions of religion result in imprisonment and death. Real faith is what takes suburbanites into the inner city to comfort those dying of AIDS, feed the hungry, or find homes for the homeless.

> » SECULAR IDEALS INSPIRE MANY PEOPLE TO DO GREAT
> GOOD, BUT FAITH IN ETERNAL PRINCIPLES IS WHAT
> DRIVES REAL SACRIFICE.

Real faith is an adventure.

That's why lasting change isn't possible without some understanding of the spiritual aspect of our lives. If we are truly spiritual creatures—even in part—then overlooking that essential aspect of our lives leaves us fragmented and incomplete. Without some understanding of the spiritual dimension, we will never find real contentment and peace.

Perhaps that is the single most important consideration of all.

Today people spend their lives making money only to discover all the really important things money can't buy. They trade their lives for a career, while losing the people they love the most. They live in physical luxury but then take their lives through suicide because of inner pain and torment.

Money is a good thing, and I love a nice house and car. But ultimately it means nothing if we haven't answered the most important questions of our lives.

To start your spiritual journey, here are some important directions on the map:

1. *Spend time with others who are honestly searching.* Perhaps it's a local church, prayer group, or like-minded friends. Make the effort to find people who can help you get the answers you need and encourage your spiritual growth. I'm a Christian, so naturally I recommend a good local church. You'll discover new friends—friends who don't care about your money, your status, or your career. Friends who will love you for *who* you are, not *what* you are.

2. *Look outward, not inward.* Help other people. Serve others. Albert Schweitzer said, "I don't know what your destiny will be, but one thing I know: the only ones among you who will be really happy are those who will have sought and found how to serve." Those who help others are the happiest people on the earth. It's not about you; it's about your ability to help other people. Discover that principle and your life will immediately change.

3. *Start to pray.* Praying isn't hard; it's simply talking to God. You don't have to use big words, fancy religious terms, or religious lingo. Simply talk to him as you would a friend. Share your challenges, your frustrations, and your dreams. You can pray while you drive a car, sit at your desk, or mow the lawn. Prayer is something that shouldn't be saved for "official" religious events—it's something that can happen anytime and anyplace. Prayer is your opportunity to connect to a power far greater than us. Make the connection, and then learn to listen.

4. *Take your faith seriously*. Real faith is not about candles, pretty jewelry, and stained glass windows. People of faith created the university system, built orphanages, started great libraries, encouraged learning, birthed hospitals, and every day help millions devastated by hurricanes, famines, and disasters of all kinds. When you realize that your life has meaning, you suddenly have a reason to live a life of purpose. One of our greatest desires is to live a life of significance, and we want to make a genuine difference in the world.

Jolt your preconceived notions about God. Faith affects us at the core of our being, and that's why it is so instrumental to our personal change. A hundred years from now it won't matter so much that you increased quarterly profits, doubled sales, lost weight, or bought a lake house. What will matter is what you left behind in the lives of people. If we want to change the world, we have to start by changing our spiritual outlook.

We don't have all the answers, but we are connected to a God who does.

REVIEW
Jolt Your Heart

Consider the importance of personal cheerleaders, accountability partners, changing perspective, and your relationship with God.

1. Find your own personal cheerleaders. Who could motivate you to greater levels of excellence?
2. If you're struggling with a particular personal challenge, list potential accountability partners. Begin interviewing people you believe would be good partners in sharing dreams and in holding each other accountable. Or find someone who will agree to hold you accountable.
3. What can I do to change my perception? How can I increase my personal value to others through the use of positive perception?
4. How can I . . .

   - increase my potential through better thinking?
   - maximize my gifts and skills through strategic thinking?
   - multiply my options through creative thinking?
   - overcome defeat and obstacles through real positive thinking?
   - experience success through long-range thinking?

Make a commitment today to deepening your relationship with God. Find areas where you can immediately grow, such as attending church, meeting with a study group, taking a class, reading books on the subject, and so on.

JOLT
YOUR
FUTURE

ELIMINATE DESTRUCTIVE DISTRACTIONS

Releasing Negative Baggage

Keep your mind off the things you don't want by keeping it on the things you do want.
—W. CLEMENT STONE, MOTIVATIONAL EXPERT

Sometimes you have to let go to see if there was anything worth holding on to.
—ANONYMOUS

We live in a culture of distraction. Everywhere we turn, we are bombarded by the noise of radio and television, mobile phones, computers, social networking, and music and video players—not to mention video screens in gas pumps and elevators and more. It occurred to me some time ago that there are few places in the United States where you can't receive a wireless signal of some type—either a satellite signal, a radio or TV station, a cell phone transmission, or a wireless computer connection. We are bathed in frequencies, signals, and transmissions.

It's not much better with our personal schedules. Remember when children used to actually play? Now kids are scheduled from dawn to dusk—school, soccer practice, music practice, church youth groups, and more. The term "soccer mom" has become almost synonymous with suburban living.

At the office we have seminars, workshops, meetings, focus groups, team gatherings—there is rarely a time when we have a moment to ourselves.

And can we talk about social networking for a minute? Yes, in many cases it's very convenient, but people popping up on your computer screen all day wanting to talk may be the single biggest distraction in offices today. It's become the number one messaging source for younger people—far more than e-mail. But there's no question that if you don't turn that thing off occasionally, it can drain hours at a time.

In his remarkable book *The Answer to How Is Yes: Acting on What Matters*, Peter Block said:

> It is entirely possible to spend our days engaged in activities that work well for us and achieve our objectives, and still wonder whether we are really making a difference in the world. My premise is that this culture, and we as members of it, have yielded too easily to what is doable and practical and popular. In the process, we have sacrificed the pursuit of what is in our hearts. We find ourselves giving in to our doubts, and settling for what we know how to do, or can soon learn how to do, instead of pursuing what most matters to us and living with the adventure and anxiety that this requires. (1)

We live days and nights filled with activities that are ultimately unfulfilling. We have crammed our lives with to-do lists and yet aren't accomplishing our dreams. We have goals but no great victory.

Much of this comes from the power of distractions—things that fill our time but leave us empty and cold. They give us the immediate feeling of accomplishment but keep us from experiencing authentic change.

In the book *Good to Great*, author Jim Collins wrote: "The real path to greatness, it turns out, requires simplicity and diligence. It requires clarity, not instant illumination. It demands each of us to focus on what is vital and to eliminate all of the extraneous distractions."

» MOST OF US LIVE UNDER THE BONDAGE OF THE URGENT.

We have phone calls to return, appointments to reach, goals to achieve, meetings to get to, e-mails to answer, and reports to finish. Our days are filled with an unrelenting barrage of everything—all of which seems so important at the time. I have this "thing" about my e-mail in-box. There's a little voice inside me that says, "You have to deal with every e-mail in your in-box by 5 p.m." No matter how trivial, I'll push aside writing a book, developing a great idea, or working on a significant project, just to get that e-mail cleared off. Because it's in front of me, it seems like something I just *have* to finish.

This chapter is about spending less time on what we perceive to be urgent and more time on what really matters.

Let that thought sink in for a moment.

Most of the "urgent" things in our lives are really what other people consider important. Someone wants us to return his phone call, make an appointment, or respond to an e-mail. Look around you at this moment. Are most of the things that are crushing your life really that urgent to you, or are they things that *other people* consider urgent? I finally noticed that when I don't deal with all my e-mails, the world doesn't come to an end. In fact, I recently had a computer malfunction and lost my e-mails from the two previous days. Gone, deleted, erased, rubbed out, cancelled, obliterated, disappeared.

I was horrified. I was in the middle of a couple of big projects and had no idea who those e-mails were from or what they were about. Who did I need to get back to? What should I do? I had no idea.

I started shaking. I needed a "fix" for my e-mail habit.

But guess what? A day went by, and then another, and then another. Nothing happened. Not dealing with those e-mails had no impact at all. My world didn't come crashing down, and my career didn't end.

I realized those e-mails were "urgent" but not important.

Since that time, I've literally reevaluated my life based on that principle. I've made a concerted effort to eliminate as many distractions as possible in order to focus more effectively on what's really important in my life.

How do we eliminate the real distractions?

First of all, understand which distractions do the most damage in your life. Distractions come in all shapes and sizes, from leisure activities like watching football on television, to personal issues from your past, to immediate challenges that disturb your life and pull vital resources and time away from what's really important.

ELIMINATE DISTRACTIONS FROM YOUR PAST THROUGH FORGIVENESS

Over the years, I've heard thousands of protests.

> "But Phil—you just don't know what my father did to me."
> "When my partner sold my business, I lost everything."
> "I can never forgive that offense—it's just too great."
> "As long as she never acknowledges fault, I can never forgive."
> "It's just too difficult because the hurt goes too deep."

There is nothing that cannot be forgiven. Forgiveness is the only real beginning to complete healing of yourself or a relationship. Keep in mind these important principles:

Forgiveness does not make what happened right.

By forgiving someone, you're not saying that what was done to you never happened or wasn't wrong. Evil is evil. When people are betrayed, wronged, or hurt in any way, the act of forgiveness doesn't make what happened right or as though it never happened. What happened is still wrong. You've just made the decision to not let it gain control of your life. You are taking back your future and attempting to restore the relationship.

If the other person refuses to acknowledge what happened, or refuses to acknowledge that it was wrong, it still can and should be forgiven. Forgiveness doesn't depend on the other person; it depends on you.

Forgiveness matters, even if the offending party refuses to admit guilt.

I know a woman who experienced horrible sexual abuse by her father for years. Because of an illness, her mother had grown weak, and, as a result, her father began preying on her for sexual gratification. Not only was it a devastating experience that continued until her teenage years, but since that time, her father has refused to admit guilt. In fact, part of her difficulty finding healing from the abuse is her father's refusal to acknowledge that it happened at all. After finally running away from home, the woman went through a series of failed marriages, and it wasn't until she experienced a spiritual transformation that she began the long road to healing from the years of abuse and neglect.

In the process of her healing, she realized that she needed to forgive her father. In spite of his refusal to take responsibility for those years of horrible cruelty, she made the difficult decision to forgive him. He continues to act as if nothing happened, but in spite of his refusal to face the truth, she has found freedom in her ability to forgive.

Don't wait for the other person to acknowledge guilt or admit wrongdoing. In fact, when you forgive some people, they'll despise you even more. But by forgiving them, you're letting the pain and hurt go and moving forward with your life. Some people have waited their entire lives for another person to admit he or she was wrong, but by doing so, they've placed their future in someone else's hands.

> » **IF YOU DON'T TAKE CONTROL OF YOUR OWN LIFE, YOU'LL ALWAYS BE AT THE MERCY OF SOMEONE ELSE WHO WILL.**

Forgiveness can be a powerful tool in healing a relationship.

Many people can never fully face the truth without someone opening the door of forgiveness. Perhaps they don't feel worthy, or perhaps they understand that what they did was wrong but don't have the courage to step forward to ask to be forgiven. Your acting first opens that door and allows them to reach out and find mercy and understanding.

Forgiveness is easier when you realize that we all need to be forgiven.

The fact is, all of us have made mistakes, hurt people, and done stupid things in our lives, and few of us can claim the moral high ground in relationships. When you have difficulty forgiving someone, just look back at things you've done that need forgiveness, and suddenly the offense against you starts to look a little more forgivable.

More than with any other religious tradition, the core of Christianity is about forgiveness. Because God has forgiven us, we are called to forgive other people. Whatever faith tradition you might be from—or no tradition at all—we can learn something from this powerful Christian principle. Because God desired a relationship with us so strongly, he was willing to allow Jesus to die on a cross as the sacrifice that would bridge the gap and heal the rift. A holy God died in order that we might be forgiven. It's the most powerful story in history, and the lesson has transformed millions of lives.

We have been forgiven, and therefore, we have the ability to forgive.

Learn to forgive yourself.

Are you carrying the baggage of blunders from your past? Have you hurt someone, acted without thinking, or damaged a relationship? Perhaps you can't even contact that person anymore and carry the burden of that terrible mistake. I talked with a man who had cheated a friend in business early in his career, and his friend had died in the intervening years. The man desperately wanted to be forgiven for his mistake, but with his old friend having died, he had nowhere to turn. He had to learn to forgive himself and move on with his life.

Don't let the pain of your past eat at you like a cancer. No matter what you've done or whom you've hurt, true healing and wholeness can never begin without the first step toward forgiveness.

The power of forgiveness can transform your life and eliminate the most painful, difficult, and challenging distractions you will ever face.

ELIMINATE DISTRACTIONS FROM
YOUR PRESENT THROUGH COMMITMENT

Unless commitment is made, there are only promises and hopes . . . but no plans.
—PETER DRUCKER, BUSINESS STRATEGIST AND WRITER

Another key to eliminating distractions is *commitment*. Commitment keeps you focused on a worthy goal, and that process alone is a tremendous help in eliminating distractions. I've discovered that the greatest opening for a distraction is not being committed to something better.

When things at the office slow down, people invariably get into trouble. One man who destroyed his marriage by having an affair with his secretary told me, "I had worked with that secretary for years, and the thought of an affair never crossed my mind—until business slowed down. When I lost my focus on the company, I began to notice her in a different way. Suddenly I became involved in a romantic distraction that eventually shattered my marriage."

Eyes wander when someone loses sight of a clearly defined goal.

Human resources executives tell me that the times when employees are mostly likely to be distracted by the Internet are during times when intensity is low—often between major projects, when things have slowed down at the office. During those times, companies lose billions in productivity from distracted and uncommitted employees.

I've seen organizations fall apart as employees lost their commitment to a vision and started getting distracted. It's amazing that in cases of office affairs, embezzling, cheating, or other problems, how often they start from a simple lack of commitment. Losing sight of a common vision opens the deadly door to distraction.

What are you committed to? A successful career? A strong family? A growing company? A better job? Raising great children? Stronger leadership? A specific project or task? Whatever it is, your commitment is a key to guarding against distraction.

How can you stay committed? First, make a public announcement. Put yourself on the spot. Write a letter to someone you respect, announce the project to your employees, or share your vision with a friend or coworker. The threat of embarrassment is a powerful tool to help keep you committed. Burn the trail behind you so you can't go back.

Spanish explorer Cortez, after arriving in the New World, took his crew off their great sailing ships and then set the ships on fire as the crew watched in horror. That single act sealed their commitment to explore the new territory and ensured they could never give in or go back. Having no alternative is a marvelous way of helping eliminate distractions.

I love painting myself into a corner. I've learned that there is something exhilarating about the adrenaline that flows as a deadline nears. Although I don't necessarily recommend this to others, I often wait until the last minute when there is no time and no alternative to finishing a project.

Nothing increases commitment like the threat of failure or the risk of embarrassment.

*Attention is one of the most valuable modern resources. If we waste it on
frivolous communication, we will have nothing left when we really need it.*
—JOHN FREEMAN, *THE TYRANNY OF E-MAIL*

Distractions—they drain your energy, blur your focus, and disrupt your
momentum. Projects fail, companies collapse, and marriages are damaged
because of the way distractions deplete resources and destroy relationships.
When I reach the end of my time on the earth, I hope to look back on a life of
significance and achievement, instead of an impotent life bled dry from the
distraction of things that added nothing to the value of my existence.

Distractions drain and take away value. Focus adds value. Eliminate
destructive distractions and prepare for a life of significance.

FAILURE IS THE KEY TO SUCCESS

Mistakes Are Just Part of the Process

You always pass failure on the way to success.

—MICKEY ROONEY, ACTOR

*Many of life's failures are people who did not realize
how close they were to success when they gave up.*

—THOMAS A. EDISON, INVENTOR

W e live in a culture of success. America celebrates winners and despises losers. We even call winners "stars." Star athletes, movie stars, TV stars, all-stars. A star reporter recently called the winners of a state spelling bee the "stars of the written word."

But anyone who has experienced success of any kind has also experienced failure. Real failure is the proving ground and training camp for success, and yet most people don't know how to learn from their mistakes. As motivational teacher Tony Robbins said, "Success truly is the result of good judgment. Good judgment is the result of experience, and experience is often the result of bad judgment!"

The greater the failure, the greater the opportunity to learn. But first we must realize the teaching potential of our mistakes and commit to an attitude of learning, growing, and changing from our failure.

*I am not discouraged, because every wrong attempt
discarded is another step forward.*

—THOMAS A. EDISON

Whenever I fall short, I'm reminded of Thomas Edison, the inventor of the lightbulb, as well as many other inventions that have changed modern society. At only twenty years old, he set up his laboratory in Menlo Park, New Jersey, and became a full-time inventor. At any given time, he and his team were working on as many as forty different projects and applied for more than four hundred patents a year. His feverish work schedule and productivity caused the local citizens to dub him the "wizard of Menlo Park."

But Edison wasn't always successful. He struggled with many of his inventions, but in spite of embarrassing failure after failure, he refused to give up. Edison was driven to succeed in spite of obstacles of all kinds. Often ridiculed for his perseverance, he attempted more than ten thousand experiments before he finally invented the incandescent lightbulb in 1879.

> *I have not failed. I've just found 10,000 ways that won't work.*
> —THOMAS A. EDISON, INVENTOR

We must stop labeling failure as negative. There are no real failures—only options. Some options work, and others don't.

In the journey of change, I've discovered that most people and organizations fail for one of four reasons: situations, emotions, motivation, or knowledge.

SITUATIONS

> *To avoid situations in which you might make mistakes*
> *may be the biggest mistake of all.*
> —PETER MCWILLIAMS, WRITER

Many people are trapped by dead-end situations they feel are impossible to change. An executive who's been forced into a meaningless job due to political maneuvering from a rival or laid off because of downsizing is a good example. Others are: a single mom carrying the burden of raising kids and making a living all by herself, a man or woman left devastated by an unfaithful spouse, and a retiree on a fixed income.

» **THERE ARE THOUSANDS OF WAYS LEADERS, MANAGERS, AND OTHERS CAN FEEL THAT THEIR PARTICULAR SITUATION HAS TURNED INTO A PRISON.**

In the 1980s, I worked with a client who was sponsoring a weekly national television program. I was asked to direct the program, and an excellent executive was named the producer. We spent six months developing the show—designing the set, hiring the crew, writing scripts, and promoting the program. The producer worked hard, and we were on track for a really exciting TV series. But about three weeks before the first broadcast, the client decided he wanted a relative to produce the program, so my friend was pulled from his producer's position and sent to manage the organization's regional office in another state.

He was trapped. It had nothing to do with his performance, and it wasn't even personal. Nepotism happens, and my friend was caught in its wake. But whatever the reason, he had to make a decision to leave the company or be trapped in a situation out of his control.

We will either find a way, or make one.
—HANNIBAL, CARTHAGINIAN GENERAL,
  LEADER OF THE FAMOUS MARCH ACROSS THE ALPS

You may feel trapped by your financial situation. Perhaps you'd like to go back to college but just can't afford it. You might like to change jobs or positions but feel trapped by your salary. I know many executives who feel ensnared by their retirement program. They've spent so many years at the company that—even though fantastic opportunities are available elsewhere—they just don't want to take the chance of risking the loss of benefits.

You may feel trapped by a physical handicap. If you're in a wheelchair, hearing impaired, or are limited by any other physical situation, obviously you have a different set of challenges than others and have to deal with that state of affairs.

The secret to overcoming what I call "situational failure" is to divide your circumstances into two groups: situations you can change and situations you can't change. I believe nearly everything can be changed or at least approached in a different way, but sometimes they can't be changed *right now*. Certain things take time, and we have to consider that as we attempt any serious change.

Make up your lists. Start with the situations you can't change right now or ever: physical handicaps, financial situations, geographic locations, family issues, age, and so forth.

Then make a list of situations you *can* change: your job, schedule, location, education, skills, friends or associates, self-confidence, and so on.

What can and cannot change is different for every person, but knowing the difference between the items on each list is critical.

Some situations are real. They can't be changed, and no matter how much we dream, hope, and wish, we can't change those circumstances. So stop wasting your time. Focus on the situations you can change, and start from there.

Far too many people fail—and continue to fail—because they're trying to change a situation that simply can't be altered. Stop banging your head against a wall and start practicing realistic thinking. See immovable obstacles for what they are and concentrate your energy, time, and effort on another area. Ignore the things you can't change and start focusing on the situations you can, and the opportunities will begin to reveal themselves.

You can't wait for inspiration, you have to go after it with a club.
—JACK LONDON, NOVELIST

EMOTIONS

The second area where most people fail is emotions. Human beings are highly emotional creatures. We have extremely developed, finely tuned, complex emotions, and our ability to be excited, laugh, cry, feel depressed, and more, sometimes creates a turmoil of conflicted feelings inside us.

While emotions are a gauge for how we feel, we cannot effectively base decisions on emotions. Ask an Olympic athlete, a concert musician, a research scientist, a professional race car driver—anyone who has to perform at the top of his game—and you'll find that much of his time is spent overriding his emotions.

"I don't feel like working today."
"I'm a little depressed."
"I'm just not in the mood."
"I just don't feel up to it."

Let those emotions take charge of your life and you'll never accomplish anything at all.

» **EMOTIONS DO PLAY AN IMPORTANT ROLE IN OUR LIVES. THE KEY IS NOT LETTING THEM CONTROL US.**

On the other hand, listening to your emotions in order to get at the core of what's bothering you can help you turn them into very revealing indicators of your condition. For instance, let's look at a couple of the statements above once again.

I don't feel like working today. Think about it for a moment. *Why* don't you feel like working? Did you stay up too late last night? Perhaps you need to change your schedule. Are you eating well? Perhaps you need to adjust your diet or food intake. Not motivated? Listen to a motivational program, read a good book, exercise, or spend some time with an encouraging friend.

I'm a little depressed. Are you getting enough relaxation? Have you taken a vacation lately? Coaches and personal trainers tell me that our moods generally swing up after exercise, so perhaps you're not getting enough exercise . Get back into an exercise program, and get into shape. Are you intimidated about the big meeting? Perhaps you need to be better prepared and do a little more homework.

You simply cannot give your life over to your emotions. They will delay you, stop you, or create detours on your journey of change.

> *I do not understand what I do. For what I want*
> *to do I do not do, but what I hate I do.*
> —ROMANS 7:15 NIV

One area worth mentioning is just how toxic certain emotions can be, particularly over the long haul. In his fascinating book *Deadly Emotions*, medical doctor and nutrition expert Don Colbert details how what you feel emotionally becomes how you feel physically. Research is showing stronger and stronger connections between our minds and bodies and how our emotions can create serious physical problems and difficulties. Dr. Colbert states,

"If a person keeps stuffing toxic emotions year after year, the day *will* come when those buried emotions come pouring out" (31).

Emotions like anger, bitterness, hostility, resentment, self-hatred, anxiety, and more can lead to many health problems, such as hypertension, coronary artery disease, autoimmune disorders, arthritis, panic attacks, heart palpitations, and tension and migraine headaches. Dr. Colbert believes that about 20 percent of the general population have levels of hostility that are high enough to be dangerous to their health—that's one out of five people!

We've all seen executives who are almost always angry, upset, and stressed-out. I directed a music video a few years ago for a major record label in Los Angeles, and the producer from the studio's music video division was a man in his forties who never stopped screaming. When I met him, I was stunned. If he wasn't screaming at me, he was screaming at someone on his cell phone. I discovered it was impossible for him to do two things: talk in a normal voice and construct a sentence without a four-letter word. Every moment of every day, he was angry, upset, or stressed-out.

When we shot the video on the East Coast, he was determined to be there to make sure I didn't mess things up. Sure enough, he showed up with an attitude. Most of the day, he sat in his chair behind me on the set, screaming at other people on his cell phone. Forget the fact that no one I met during the entire project respected him or enjoyed working with him. But just as important, I imagine that man doesn't have long to go before all that intensity and stress cause something physical to break down.

Keep your emotions in check. Don't become a robot and fight your feelings, because emotions are a big part of what makes us human. Ignoring our feelings creates just as much a problem in the long run, so we need to acknowledge them and understand their influence. But also understand where they come from, and don't let them control your life.

MOTIVATION

Your motivation? Your motivation is your pay packet on Friday.
Now get on with it.
—NOEL COWARD, PLAYWRIGHT

A key ingredient of motivation is sharing your journey with others. Many people fail for lack of motivation, and most motivation comes from outside sources. You need to be encouraged, applauded, and valued on a regular basis because motivation is the intangible element that allows you to break through barriers and limitations. When you've reached the end of your knowledge about a problem, run out of tools and options, or lost your way, motivation is what can get you through.

» **IN BUSINESS AND IN LIFE, VERY OFTEN SHEER MOTIVATION OVERCOMES LACK OF KNOWLEDGE, RESOURCES, AND SKILL.**

Working in the entertainment industry, I see plenty of young people with an intense motivation to make a movie. In some extreme cases, they've never been to Hollywood, have no filmmaking skills, no experience, and no contacts with anyone in that world. In a few cases, all they have is motivation, but sometimes that is enough.

Stay motivated. Don't let a lack of inspiration deprive you of your dream. Surround yourself with people who will speak possibility into your life.

KNOWLEDGE

Stupid is forever, ignorance can be fixed.
—DON WOOD, WRITER

Far too often, people don't think realistically, get the information they need, or find the right expertise. Edison failed many times, but his eventual success didn't come from dumb luck—it came from preparation. Too many people today undervalue knowledge.

Because computers allow us to try and fail so many times, we refuse to take the time to read the manual. Because we feel so rushed, we refuse to stop and find out what we really need to know. Because young people are pressured into careers, they often don't see the value in spending time getting a good education.

When I was a kid, I idolized the Green Bay Packers. For me, they were the ultimate football team. Coached by the legendary Vince Lombardi and quarterbacked by Bart Starr, in my eyes there wasn't anything those players couldn't do. Lombardi took them to the highest levels of excellence, but no matter how many championships they won or trophies they took home, Lombardi never stopped practicing the fundamentals—the basics that can make or break a champion.

> *Learn the fundamentals of the game and stick to them.*
> *Band-Aid remedies never last.*
> —JACK NICKLAUS, PROFESSIONAL GOLF CHAMPION

Every day people are promoted out of their level of competence. But they don't keep up with the growing wealth of knowledge about leadership and business, and sooner or later, they are exposed. Failure happens when your knowledge doesn't keep up with your position.

> *Would you like me to give you a formula for success? It's quite simple, really.*
> *Double your rate of failure.*
> —THOMAS J. WATSON, FOUNDER OF IBM

Jolt your attitude toward failure. Failure is simply a potential result. Every attempt can yield different results, and some work better than others.

You are not a failure—you are part of the process, and every outcome is another step on the road to eventual success. Without failure, change is never possible and success can never be achieved.

Embrace it. Learn from it. Turn your failures into knowledge and your knowledge into success.

GET OVER YOURSELF!

It Is Not About You

The smaller the mind the greater the conceit.

—AESOP (620 BC–560 BC)

Pride goes before destruction, and a haughty spirit before a fall.

—PROVERBS 16:18 NKJV

In the 2004 Summer Olympics in Greece, the United States Olympic basketball team sported some of the great players of the game, and coach Larry Brown was one of the most experienced coaches in the country. The American players were outstanding athletes and could play at a level few outside the United States have ever achieved. But in spite of their remarkable individual skills and talent, by the time the final buzzer went off, the U.S. Olympic basketball team could do no better than the bronze medal.

Teams from Argentina and Italy with less individual talent beat us decisively. Everybody likes a star, but in a *team* sport, success comes more from teamwork than from individual talent. The United States was unable to win the gold because the players—as talented as they were—couldn't work together as a team. Each player came from a different background, a different style of play, with different priorities, and as a unit they were unable to gel when they needed it most.

From this point on, stop thinking about life as an individual event, and start looking at your life and career as a team sport. Your company is filled with other team members. Your family is a team. You form a team with your clients or customers. To accomplish anything of significance in today's economy, we have to work as a team.

Historians have revealed that many of the greatest artists and leaders of the past actually accomplished their greatest work as a team. When I first visited the Sistine Chapel in Rome and looked in awe and wonder at Michelangelo's magnificent ceiling, I assumed he had done it all by himself. I pictured him alone on the scaffolding—as in the movies—slaving away, with occasional trips down the ladder to replenish his paints.

But since that time, I've learned how the great artist created a team of brilliant assistants—artists and artisans in their own right—who helped him in a vast number of ways. They found the best raw materials needed to make the finest paints and knew how to mix them for the best results. He had assistants to help him outline the major scenes, others to help fill in, and still others who used their skills with various details of the project. Art historians tell us that most of the major painters of the period set up schools and worked with various students and assistants to accomplish their work. In fact, I walked through a museum recently in Washington, D.C., and viewed a painting that was credited to the school rather than the artist. A great artist painted it, but there was no way to be sure how much he painted and how much his students completed.

It reminds me of how animated cartoons and feature films are created today. After you watch the next major animated feature at your local theater, stay in your seat and watch the credits for the staggering number of gifted artists and professionals who worked on the project. Some do the rough drawings, others outline the scenes, others fill in the color, still others handle the details—not to mention the sound effects, voices, and music. None of this information detracts from the genius of the great artists throughout history. But it does reinforce the critical importance of teams.

» **TECHNOLOGY, POLITICS, BUSINESS, GLOBALIZATION, MEDIA, AND CULTURE HAVE GROWN SO COMPLEX AND MULTILAYERED, IT'S NEARLY IMPOSSIBLE FOR A SINGLE PERSON TO REACH THE HIGHEST LEVELS OF ACHIEVEMENT.**

Does that take anything away from the importance of the individual? Absolutely not. Individuals are the fuel that makes progress possible. Individuals are the core of the enterprise. But joined together through relationships, anything is possible.

The power of relationships can open doors you could never open on your own. It can provide favor when money or resources aren't enough, and it can help you find the answers you desperately need.

The key to unlocking openness at work is to teach people to give up having to be in agreement. We think agreement is so important. Who cares? You have to bring paradoxes, conflicts, and dilemmas out in the open, so collectively we can be more intelligent than we can be individually.
—PETER SENGE, M.I.T. PROFESSOR

Although most of this book is focused on increasing your individual sense of accomplishment, potential for success, and ability to change, we must also keep ourselves in perspective. We are relatively small cogs in a much bigger picture, and it will take cooperation, networking, and people skills to reach the next level in our lives.

» **I HAVE NOTHING AGAINST SELF-ESTEEM, BUT I HAVE TO ADMIT, WE'VE COME THROUGH A PERIOD WHERE SELF-ESTEEM TEACHING BECAME EXCESSIVE.**

People became obsessed with positive self-esteem, and it permeated business, education, and communities. It all began back in 1969, when psychologist Nathaniel Branden published a highly acclaimed paper called "The Psychology of Self-Esteem." He argued that "feelings of self-esteem were the key to success in life," and his idea soon became the hot new thing in education. At the apex of the craze, the California legislature even established a "Self-Esteem Task Force" for the state's schools.

But the problem with teaching self-esteem? It doesn't work.

Writing in the *Wall Street Journal* about the fifteen thousand studies the movement generated, Kay Hymowitz concluded:

And what do they show? That high self-esteem doesn't improve grades, reduce anti-social behavior, deter alcohol drinking or do much of anything good for kids. In fact, telling kids how smart they are can be counterproductive. Many children who are convinced that they are little geniuses tend not to put much effort into their work. Others are troubled by the latent anxiety of adults who feel it necessary to praise them constantly.

The book *NurtureShock*, by Po Bronson and Ashley Merryman, may put the final nail in the coffin of the self-esteem movement. For instance, as Hymowitz pointed out, the book reveals that

> drop-out programs [based on self-esteem] don't work. Neither do anti-drug programs. The most popular of them, D.A.R.E. (Drug Abuse Resistance Education), developed in 1983 by the Los Angeles Police Department, has become a more familiar sight in American schools than algebra class. By 2000, 80% of American school districts were using D.A.R.E. materials in some form. Now, after extensive study, comes the news: The program has no long-term, and only mild short-term, effects. Oh, and those tests that school districts use to determine giftedness in young children? They're just about useless.

When people focus excessively on themselves, it damages the potential of the greater project. My wife and I were leaders of our local high school choir parent boosters organization. The music program was national caliber, and the four choirs from the school traveled extensively, competing and performing nationwide. As a result, they needed an unusually high-level fund-raising program, and the parent boosters were the driving force behind it. Kathleen and I weren't in leadership roles very long before we realized the biggest challenge we faced was from a small handful of parents who thought little about the overall program and only about themselves.

Every project we discussed, they viewed not through the lens of the choir but through the lens of their particular family. All they cared about was their son or daughter, and they had little concern for the overall program. As a result, I had to spend the vast majority of my time fixing the problems they caused, bandaging the hurts they inflicted on other families, and repairing the damage to the program. The great majority of the parents thought in terms of the choir and were a joy to work with, but when only a few parents became self-centered, it created problems that grew difficult to control.

CONNECTING WORKS

One of the least understood and most powerful concepts in life is the power of connecting and networking. When you discover the awesome influence of "we," you'll see doors open, walls falling, and obstacles disappearing. You can never accomplish as much individually as you can with connections.

Realize that there are two types of networking.

There is networking to develop your personal relationships, and there is networking to connect other people. Both interrelate, and both will benefit you in different ways. Truthfully, I've personally received more benefit from helping other people than I have from networking for myself directly.

It's about relationship building.

Real networking is about building genuine friendships, not just building blocks to your career. Care about the people. You've heard the phrase, "People don't care how much you know until they know how much you care," and it's exactly right. Years ago, the vice president for a major corporation told me, "If you're genuinely interested in a client's family, he'll be a client for life." The key word is *genuine*. It's all about authenticity. People aren't stupid, and they can detect when you don't really care.

Don't focus on you.

Be genuinely interested in the project, the problem, or the person. Do it for the right reasons. The old model is most evident in the TV series *The Sopranos*. Sure they get their friends jobs in construction, but once they do, they just sit around the construction site in lounge chairs, drinking beer. Nothing really positive happens. They make the money, but they don't learn, grow, increase their skill level, or add value to the company. In the new networking paradigm, the person has to be right, you have to be right, and the project has to be right.

Start a network archive.

Consciously think about everyone you know, their particular skills, and how they connect. When I was a young director, I made a list of people I enjoyed working with, and I thought that one day, whenever I might get a big project, I'm bringing them with me. It was a good list, and ever since then I've continued the habit. Only today I use a computer-based contact system for the same thing. Now when I hear about an opportunity, I can immediately find a good candidate in my contact list.

Trade information with people.

Trade business cards at conferences and meetings, keep them organized, and put them in your contact manager. Don't be obnoxious, but graciously offer people your cards and ask for theirs. It's a fantastic way to build relationships and keep track of contact information.

When you connect people, make a good match.

Consider their career standing, experience, and personal habits and skills. All of these things become critical for making solid connections work. All it takes is one bad match and people will begin avoiding you. Make sure whenever you connect two people for a project, they are as compatible as possible.

> *The meeting of two personalities is like the contact of two chemical substances: if there is any reaction, both are transformed.*
> —CARL JUNG, PSYCHIATRIST

Meeting people is the heart and soul of networking. My father had the ability to make friends more easily than anyone I've ever known. One day we were shopping, and while my mom was looking at dresses, my dad struck up a conversation with a motorcycle cop outside the store. Within minutes, not only was my dad in conversation with the motorcycle cop, but he was also using the cop's police radio to chat with the local police chief back at the station. My dad could start a conversation with anyone, anytime and anyplace.

Finally, a few closing thoughts about networking:

Don't keep a balance sheet.

Sometimes you'll connect people for a great project that becomes a success, but they'll leave you out in the cold. For some reason, people don't always reciprocate and pay back favors. Life isn't always fair, but don't let that stop you and don't let it destroy your motivation. Even if you get abused four out of five times, one positive experience will still be worth it.

Become a person who makes things happen.

Men and women will always be drawn to the leaders who can get things done. The minute you miss a deadline, drop the ball, or fail, people will subtly start avoiding you, but "action" people are magnets. Michael Jordan was a clutch basketball player. When the clock was ticking, the team was behind, and the chips were down, everyone had confidence that if there was time for one last shot, Michael could make it. He was the epitome of the "go-to" guy because he knew how to make things happen.

In the same way, establish a personal reputation that, no matter what, you can make things happen. Be a game changer.

Learn the art of motivation.

Give people hope. Most people you meet are frustrated, are upset, or have given up on life. But if you can motivate them, you can build a network that can accomplish anything. Look around your company and you'll see how few people are really motivators. Most employees, managers, and executives are only concerned about "what's in it for me." They cover their own backsides, think only about themselves, and rarely try to make a difference for others. If you can become a motivator, your influence in the company will skyrocket.

Collaboration is multiplication.
—JOHN C. MAXWELL, AUTHOR

Understand the power of teams.

Even the Lone Ranger, Roy Rogers, Batman, and the Green Hornet all had one thing in common—they worked with a sidekick. Tonto, Dale Evans,

Robin, and Kato were the relationships that made each of those teams work.

You don't have to do it yourself. Stop thinking about "you" and start thinking about "we." Multiply your impact and increase your effectiveness.

THE POWER OF SOLVING PROBLEMS

Taking your eyes off yourself is the first step to real vision. That's why one of the greatest keys to becoming successful is to do something for someone else. In the chapter on generosity we discussed giving, but let me take that a step further:

Problem solving may be the single most important task you will ever undertake. Solve someone else's problem and it will change your life.

Want to be rich? Become more valuable to others.

Want to move up in the company? Become indispensable.

Solving problems is what makes you more precious and essential in today's workplace.

The bigger the problems you solve, the more valuable you become.

I have a business partner and close friend named Ralph Winter. Ralph produces major blockbuster movies, and he's very good at it. He's produced *Star Trek*, *Mighty Joe Young*, *Inspector Gadget*, Tim Burton's *Planet of the Apes*, *X-Men*, *X2*, *Wolverine*, and *The Fantastic Four*.

Ralph is an expert at solving problems, and because he's so good, studios are willing to compensate him accordingly. Ralph has a reputation that when a major special effects extravaganza is out of control, he's the man to get it back on track. I've seen him get the call when a major high-budget movie was in production and spinning out of sight. He would fly to the location, bring in his team, rework the budget and shooting schedule, reassure nervous actors and crew, and calm down frantic studio executives.

In a world where major movies cost more than $100 million, Ralph solves expensive problems. As a result, he's very valuable.

» IT'S NOT ABOUT YOU. IT'S ABOUT SOLVING PROBLEMS.

I pay my housekeeper one salary, but I pay my attorney another salary altogether because my attorney solves bigger problems. Learn to solve bigger problems and you'll never again need to worry about salary, hourly rates, fees, or income.

When you solve problems, someone is watching. Chances are, the president, CEO, client, or other person significant to your future is watching you solve problems. And the bigger the problem, the bigger the audience.

Effective problem solving is a key to becoming a more effective part of the team, building relationships, getting noticed, and moving up the ladder. Stop thinking about your needs, your wants, and your troubles.

Look for a big problem to solve and get with it.

LEAVE A LEGACY OF CHANGE

How Will You Be Remembered?

The legacy of heroes is the memory of a great name and the inheritance of a great example.
—BENJAMIN DISRAELI, BRITISH PRIME MINISTER AND NOVELIST

LORD, *remind me how brief my time on earth will be. Remind me that my days are numbered, and that my life is fleeing away.*
—PSALM 39:4 NLT

I recently asked a group of major executives and CEOs what their single greatest concern might be about their business and career. I was expecting answers like the need to pursue innovation, finding new funding and financing, building better teams, or expanding global markets. But a significant number of corporate executives I interviewed replied: "I'm concerned about what kind of legacy I leave behind."

I was reminded of the story of a very rich man's funeral. In his lifetime, he lived in luxury and made hundreds of millions of dollars. At the funeral service, one of his former associates leaned over and asked the man's business manager how much he left behind.

"All of it," the business manager replied.

When we die, we leave it all. We can't take our wealth, our property, or our accomplishments. We leave everything, and as we consider our last will and testament and what we'll leave behind, we can't forget that we'll all be leaving a legacy as well.

When that happens, what will your legacy be? Will it be a list of business successes, properties, or stocks? Throughout history, some of the richest and most influential men and women have left a great deal of money, but they've also handed down a legacy of bitterness, confusion, and discontent. They have left families torn apart by unfair treatment, abuse, scandal, selfishness, and deceit.

The kinds of problems all the money in the world can't fix.

> ## » DEATH IS THE ULTIMATE TRANSITION, THE FINAL CHANGE, THE LAST JOLT.

Others, who had far less money, left a more significant legacy. They left behind people whose lives were dramatically changed because of their impact. People who were never the same because someone passed through their lives who cared and brought them great value.

» WHAT WILL YOU LEAVE BEHIND?

This isn't a chapter intended to be read an hour before you die. The earlier you learn this lesson the better, because the more time you'll have to build your "lifetime equity" and the greater chance your life will have meaning and impact after you're gone.

Certainly financial riches are a good thing to leave behind. Designated financial gifts have built hospitals, schools, churches, and libraries. They have provided an education for those who could never have gone to college on their own. And they have allowed vast projects in underdeveloped countries to make an impact on countless people the giver never knew.

Money is good, and if you have a talent for making it, I'm your best cheerleader. By all means, build up a financial legacy that you can leave to impact lives for generations to come.

But leaving a legacy is about so much more than just money. Here are some suggestions I would urge you to consider as you think about leaving behind a heritage that really matters.

THOUGHTS ABOUT YOUR LEGACY

First, settle the ultimate questions.

In the old days they called it "being ready to meet your Maker." That sounds trite and old-fashioned, but the point is, settle the big questions of your life and search for the spiritual answers you need to find.

Remember our earlier questions: Where did I come from? Why am I here? Where am I going? What is my purpose? Take care of spiritual issues so that no matter what happens—or when it happens—you're ready for the next world. Whatever you do, don't leave those questions unanswered.

Growing up a pastor's son, I've spent many nights in hospital rooms with my dad as he comforted church members and friends who were dying. As long as I live, I will never forget the difference between people who knew where they were going and those who didn't. Time and time again, people who had a strong faith died with a sense of peace, as if they were ready for a divine appointment. But during those difficult times when my father had to be at the bedside of someone who refused to acknowledge any spiritual dimension to life, the person often died in fear and terror, with a nervous sense that there were unanswered questions and things not settled.

I don't write that to scare anyone or to trivialize serious doubts or skepticism about the supernatural or the afterlife. But whatever decision you make, please make a decision so that when your time comes, you're comfortable with the knowledge that you've wrestled with the ultimate questions of life and made a choice.

Second, spend your life investing in people.

Leaving behind buildings, monuments, or companies is a wonderful thing, and I'm all for it. In fact, if you would like to leave behind a building for me, please let me know. I'm happy to accept! But the truth is, the greatest legacy you'll ever leave is in the lives of people. Martin Luther King Jr., Gandhi, Jesus, Mother Teresa, Fred Rogers, and many more didn't leave great corporations, buildings, or property. But they will be remembered for generations to come because of the legacy they created in the lives of millions. People will always be your greatest investment, and no matter how much money you make, you can never leave enough to outweigh the influence and impact you leave when you spend your life helping other people.

> » **YOU DON'T HAVE TO BE RICH OR INFLUENTIAL TO START MAKING A DIFFERENCE.**

All it takes is the effort and desire to change someone's life. Find a younger executive to mentor, help a needy family, or take a leadership role in the life of a teen. One of the most shameful aspects of our modern culture is the tragic numbers of children growing up without a mom or a dad. Men—find a teenage boy without a father and develop a "big brother" relationship. Help that young man grow into manhood with a father figure, and share your life experience and resources with him.

In the same way, women can play an identical role for girls and young women who are growing up without mothers. I went to elementary school with a girl whose mom had died of cancer. She and her younger sister were being raised by a father who had little knowledge of the complexities of raising girls. I'll never forget how adult women in the church would make the effort to help those girls with motherly advice, teaching them things their father could never understand about becoming a woman.

The movie *The Blind Side* is the story of a poor, homeless, and uneducated teenaged boy named Michael Oher, who was given a second chance by a Memphis family. When Leigh Anne and Sean Touhy invited Michael into their home, it changed his life and theirs as well. Their unconditional love, support, and mentoring allowed him to finish high school, become an All-American offensive left tackle at the University of Mississippi, and graduate from college. He later became the number one NFL draft pick of the Baltimore Ravens.

There is someone within your reach right now who needs you to make a difference. It won't be hard once you make a habit of looking. In many ways, that's actually the key to investing in people—the ability to see. So many people go through life oblivious to the people or needs that surround them, but once you sharpen your senses toward people you can really help, you'll begin to see lives you can impact on a regular basis.

» **INVEST IN PEOPLE, AND YOUR RETURN WILL LAST FOR GENERATIONS.**

Third, be deliberate about your legacy.

Don't wait until the last minute, start planning now. What are some of the things you can leave behind as a legacy?

Books, music, a journal, great projects, buildings, students, children, inventions, breakthroughs, research, innovation, creativity, solutions, designs, money, property, investments, good advice, education, favor, networks, forgiveness, photographs, documents, a successful business, software, movies, lectures, experience, and the list goes on and on.

Your legacy can be anything that makes people realize that you left a mark and the world is a better place because you passed through. Most people limit a legacy to only money, books, or artistic works, but brainstorm about what you can leave behind—it could be nearly anything—as long as it makes a positive difference for at least one person.

» **BUT TO LEAVE SOMETHING SIGNIFICANT, YOU NEED TIME, AND THAT'S WHY IT'S CRITICAL THAT YOU START THINKING ABOUT IT NOW.**

Fourth, start small.

My daughter Bailey told me years ago that she had started keeping a journal. Every night before bedtime, she took a few minutes to write down her thoughts, ideas, and reflections on the day. As we discussed it, she remarked how much she wished her grandfather had done the same thing. He came out of a small Southern town to become a Golden Gloves boxer, World War II hero, educator, pastor—how much it would mean to her today to be able to read his reflections through the years, particularly during critical periods in his life.

You have no idea how much a simple, daily journal could mean for your children and grandchildren years from today. A personal journal is a great place to start, and it doesn't take much to begin. If you don't like to write, record it. With tiny digital recorders and voice recognition software, there's no reason you can't leave an amazing record of your life.

Fifth, learn the power of investment.

A few years ago, I read the story of a widowed public high school teacher in the Midwest who never made more than about $35,000 a year during her entire lifetime. She had no children, and when she died, the community was stunned to discover that she had left millions of dollars as a financial gift to a local college. How did she do it? Saving her money and a simple program of investing. She wasn't an investment genius and was actually quite conservative in her decisions, but with some good advice, respectable stock choices, and the power of compound interest, a meager salary was turned into a legacy of millions by the time she died. Thanks to her financial vision, for many years to come, hundreds of students will reap the benefits of that one teacher's legacy.

Chances are, most readers will already be involved in a serious investment strategy. If so, begin thinking about how to maximize a portion of your money for the purpose of making a financial difference in an educational institution, church, charity, or nonprofit organization after you're gone.

And if you don't have many financial resources, don't wait "until you have money" to invest. Begin today to put something—*anything*—into a savings account, and work from there. Learn about mutual funds, stocks, bonds, and other financial opportunities. Learn about the real estate market. I'm not a financial advisor, so I encourage you to talk with one. Check them out carefully and get recommendations from people you trust. There are a lot of con artists out there, so you can never be too careful or cautious when it comes to your money.

But do it today. Enroll in a class on financial management. Talk to your banker, accountant, or attorney. Get good advice, and discover the power of managing your finances for the best possible result.

Who is your successor? I'm not just talking about family members here. I'm always amazed at how little effort major companies make to think ahead about successors. Someone once said, "Success without a successor is failure." If you own a company, lead an organization, or run a family business, you need to plan for the transition to the next generation.

» THE HISTORY OF AMERICAN BUSINESS IS LITTERED WITH COMPANIES WHO NEVER UNDERSTOOD HOW TO MAKE A POSITIVE TRANSITION TO THE NEXT GENERATION.

Family members fight, boards argue, and executives battle over succession, and all the while drain the company of money, time, and resources.

When the founder of a nonprofit organization in the Midwest decided to step down, he considered converting the organization into a foundation. The organization was worth more than $100 million, and becoming a foundation would have assured its impact for generations. But family infighting delayed the transition for years, and the founder finally relented to family pressure and passed the organization on to his son. I'm told the nonprofit is now struggling under his poor leadership and is desperately attempting to find a new vision for the future. If it continues on its present course, the impact it could have made as a foundation may crumble as the endowment is eventually eaten away.

Sometimes founders are convinced that the only people who will ever really care about the organization are family members, and they turn away highly qualified future leaders in exchange for poorly qualified sons and daughters.

Whatever decision you make and whatever circumstances you face, start planning now. Even if you feel you have ten or fifteen years ahead of you, it's never too early to begin thinking about the transition to the next generation.

Leave a legacy! Your life on the earth will be measured by two things: what you accomplish with your life and what you accomplish with your legacy. Many well-known men and women—who accomplished great things in life— left nothing of significance after they died. In some cases, information about private excess, wrongdoing, or scandal discovered after their deaths tainted their accomplishments and left them a legacy of failure and disdain.

But many who lived unknown or modest lives created a legacy that will last for generations.

A legacy is made up of many ingredients, including vision, foresight, integrity, service, compassion, and generosity. It's about planting seeds in the lives of others that will reap harvests for many seasons in the future.

> » IF YOU'VE WRONGED OTHERS, SEEK THEIR
> FORGIVENESS. IF YOU'VE MADE MISTAKES,
> MAKE THEM RIGHT. CLEAR THE SLATE NOW,
> SO YOU'RE NOT HAUNTED BY THE THOUGHTS
> OF WHAT MIGHT HAVE BEEN.

Jolt!

In the opening scene of the legendary film *Citizen Kane*, Charles Foster Kane, played by Orson Welles, dies with the faintly whispered word "rosebud" on his lips. The entire movie becomes the intriguing story of a reporter desperately searching through Kane's past to discover the word's elusive meaning. This vastly wealthy businessman who influenced world leaders had spent his life in luxury and wealth, only to reach his deathbed with regrets and a desperate wish for the past.

Make sure your last words don't express regret or remorse. Don't leave anything unfinished.

Leave a legacy, and make your life count for eternity.

LIVE A BLOCKBUSTER LIFE

Discover the Far-Reaching Power of Influence

Philosophical purists may weep and gnash their teeth, but the fact is that movies are the most powerful cultural influence we have today.
—COLIN MCGINN, PROFESSOR OF PHILOSOPHY AT RUTGERS UNIVERSITY

Let no man imagine that he has no influence. Whoever he may be, and wherever he may be placed, the man who thinks becomes a light and a power.
—HENRY GEORGE, ECONOMIST

Kathleen and I have two incredible daughters—Kelsey and Bailey—both grown now. Because of my experience with daughters, when I think of influence, I think of Hollywood. From the time they *absolutely had to have* a Snow White dress, to now, when a smartphone has become a standard accessory, I can see the power of the media industry through many of the choices my daughters make on a daily basis.

Hollywood isn't the *entertainment* industry; it's the *influence* industry. The world of power and influence. It seems that today—like most of recorded history—nearly everyone wants it, and nowhere in the world is it more visible than in Hollywood.

Blockbuster movies are making nearly $100 million in a single weekend, and major stars are demanding $10 to $20 million per movie. Video games, websites, DVDs, and merchandising are all growth industries—and each is tied to the phenomenal success of entertainment.

Network television isn't much different. Prime-time television is spinning off programs at a record pace, creating a global television market that is dominated by American programming. In third-world countries where houses have no windows and people have no medical care, they still never miss an episode of popular network shows. Major global companies are competing to own entertainment industry assets, as the money, the prestige, and the glamour become just too difficult to pass up.

The entertainment industry in the United States represents remarkable influence. For instance, when major "event" movies, like *Spider-man, Avatar,* or *The X-Men,* premiere, an awesome marketing machine is triggered to capture a specific target audience. In many cases, the target audience is teenage boys, some even showing up dressed in superhero outfits, and all willing to stand in line for hours to catch the first exciting glimpse of a new action movie.

The ability of the movie and television industries to sell, influence, and promote is the raw power that drives audience impact. But what if we could harness that awesome power and create blockbuster lives? There's no question it could transform our personal performance, our leadership, and our future.

» **NEARLY THIRTY YEARS CONSULTING AND WRITING ON CHANGE HAS TAUGHT ME THAT THE PRINCIPLES IN THIS BOOK CAN CREATE A BLOCKBUSTER SUCCESS IN YOUR BUSINESS AND IN YOUR LIFE.**

Hollywood has always been a mysterious place full of intrigue, deals at the trendy lunch spots, and glitzy stars and starlets, and it's captured a place in the hearts of the public because it deals in fantasy and escape. In that respect, it's very different from industries such as insurance, retail, service, or transportation, and therefore few people on the outside really understand how it works.

Why is Hollywood so successful?

Because it understands the power of a good jolt. Most people think movies echo the cultural changes in society, but the fact is, movies take so long to produce, they have to begin years before they actually hit the theaters. That means producers and studio executives must be thinking about how the culture will be changing three to five years from today—particularly for major "event" movies.

Hollywood can't be caught living on last year's success. That's why so few sequels make as much money as the original. By the time the first movie is successful, the trends are changing once again.

» **CHANGE IS THE ENGINE THAT DRIVES THE MOVIE AND TELEVISION BUSINESS, AND CHANGE IS THE ENGINE THAT SHOULD DRIVE YOUR LIFE.**

The principles we've discussed in this book are your tools for achieving that change, and they can have a major impact on any person, organization, or business. They have been tested over time and have proven to be foundational principles for success—the kind of success that reaps billions at the box office and has the potential to create cultural changes as well. The kind of success that has made Hollywood famous on a global scale and can help you discover your purpose.

The key is understanding the real meaning of *power*.

THE INFLUENCE OF POWER

It takes tremendous discipline to control the influence,
the power you have over other people's lives.
—CLINT EASTWOOD, AWARD-WINNING MOVIE ACTOR AND DIRECTOR

Most dictionaries refer to *power* as "the ability to act, the capability to produce an effect, or the capacity to influence, either for good or bad." There's no question that since the beginning of the modern entertainment industry, movies and television programs have had enormous power. In fact, many would argue that the mass media has become the most powerful influence on attitudes and behavior in our culture today.

Culture critic Robert Johnston has noted that, as early as 1934, in the movie *It Happened One Night*, popular star Clark Gable acted in the movie without an undershirt to better display his physique and, thereafter, undershirt sales dropped dramatically nationwide. In fact, it was not until World War II when the military retrained men to wear undershirts that the crippled industry finally recovered.

And in 1942, when Walt Disney's animated feature *Bambi* premiered, deer hunting in America dropped from a $5.7 million business to barely $1 million. (What kid would let his dad shoot Bambi?)

Even off camera, Hollywood exerts influence, as more and more movie and television stars have become activists for a variety of causes—even testifying before Senate committees.

The power and influence movies and television exert on the public seems to grow with each passing year. Notice the frenzy at a local fast-food restaurant involved in a joint marketing campaign with a new movie release or the extensive research being done by respected organizations into the impact movie violence, sex, profanity, or even smoking has on viewers, especially children and teens.

In a recent marketing alliance, a major Hollywood studio made a deal with a soft drink company to have their movie title emblazoned on *one billion* soft drink cans. In an advertising world governed by impressions, that's a powerful strategy since not only will the soft drink buyers see the logo, but everyone who passes by the soft drink display in stores will see it as well—not to mention its presence in TV commercials and print ads.

There is no question that Hollywood understands power and influence. Whether it's the power a movie star exerts to get his or her way on a film set, or the power and influence a movie has on the public, many would agree that *power* is the currency of the entertainment business. By that standard, the entertainment industry is easily America's number one export. While we might think of agriculture, military equipment, or computer technology topping the list, the fact is, the entertainment industry exerts more influence globally than anything else this country produces.

THE POWER OF INFLUENCE

But ultimately, I'm not interested in power, I'm interested in *influence*. The media business is all about influence and the ability to change people's behavior. That's why the most successful entertainment companies and executives understand that Hollywood is not in the business of *entertainment*—it's in the business of *influence*. Even the most creative writers, directors, and producers who might disagree with such a financial perspective, acknowledge that while they might not necessarily want the viewers to purchase a product, they do want the viewers to be influenced by ideas. Liberal, conservative, religious, secular, environmental, feminist, gay—whatever—every producer has a personal worldview, and that worldview is usually expressed at some level through his or her work.

How does this relate to you and your future?

By understanding influence, you begin to understand how to impact people's behavior. But there are some critical keys to understanding the role influence plays in our lives.

Real influence is not about manipulation.

We're not trying to control people and force them to bend to our will. We want our audience, our business associates, our customers, or the greater culture to be influenced in a positive way—to make their lives better, more fulfilled, and more successful. As you learned in "Negotiating 101," when you force your opponents to comply, you may get their bodies, but you don't win their minds. And to be successful, your audience must want what you're selling, and want it from the heart.

Real influence requires integrity.

When I started directing actors, the first rule I learned was a good actor must always honestly listen to the other actors. Bad actors don't listen during a scene; they're just thinking of what line to say next. The result of that approach is cheesy, corny, and simply bad acting. One of the critical keys to being a great actor is to learn to listen effectively to the other actors in the scene. In the same way, you must be willing to honestly empathize and care for your clients and customers. A "glazed over" look during a business meeting can be spotted a mile away. You have to be sincere because sincerity can be felt. Study after study indicates that true integrity is the cornerstone of a successful personal and business life.

» SURE YOU CAN CON YOUR WAY FOR A WHILE,
BUT SOONER OR LATER (USUALLY SOONER)
IT ALWAYS CATCHES UP.

In the book *Love Is the Killer App* by Tim Sanders, chief solutions officer for Yahoo! (I love his title), Sanders shatters the theory that good business is driven by ruthless, coldhearted executives. The classic, tough, uncaring image of business is simply not true—especially if you want to inspire success—and Sanders does a brilliant job showing the difference integrity, character, and respect can make in the workplace.

The problem is, everywhere you look today you can see a lack of integrity—even in the highest and most prestigious places of business. In fact, some of this country's largest and most productive companies are collapsing due to a lack of integrity, and the ripples are being felt around the world. Sometimes it's due to financial impropriety, sometimes sexual misconduct. Still others engage in deceptive promotion and selling. There are a million ways to damage your integrity, but building it back is something else entirely. Starting today, make integrity an important priority because once you lose it, it's almost impossible to ever get it back.

Real influence is about making a positive difference in the lives of people.

When you leave a legacy of change in the lives of others, it is the most fulfilling accomplishment you will ever achieve. It's not about looking inside at your problems and challenges, it's about looking outside to help others.

Life is a great big canvas; throw all the paint on it you can.
—DANNY KAYE, FILM ACTOR AND COMEDIAN

Understanding influence is a critical foundation for blockbuster success. No matter where you are in an organization, your actions touch people's lives—either for good or bad. The jolts we've discussed in this book can change your life, and through the power of influence, they can change the lives of everyone on your team or in your company, your associates, and even your family.

Now—from this moment on, I only have three rules:

1. *Reread key chapters that describe areas you're dealing with the most.* When we were kids in elementary school, if we wrote in a library book, we were in big trouble. But I'm inviting you to make up for lost time and go back and write in this book anywhere you like—scribble in the margins,

make notes, and even draw pictures if it helps. Take a highlighter and mark specific passages that stand out for you, and note them for easy reference later. Reread chapters that you struggle with because this is a critical part of the learning process. Even after you finish the book, keep it nearby and scan your notes on a regular basis. It's one thing to read something over, but it's far better to make notes, re-scan the information regularly, and get it deep into your mind and spirit where these principles will be at your fingertips whenever you need them.

2. *Share this information on change with at least two other people.* There's an ancient oriental proverb that says, "You never really learn something until you've taught it to someone else." I believe that with all my heart. When you share new information with others, it forces you to think about it and articulate it in a practical, informative way. Don't be shy about sharing information on change because it can have a major impact on your future as well as the future of others. Begin sharing new information with friends and colleagues on a regular basis, and you'll discover fantastic insight and suggestions coming back as well. I have friends who make a regular program of reading and discussing business books. No one person can read everything, so we divide and conquer. Each of us takes a book and teaches the rest of us all about it. We still usually end up personally buying nearly everything anyway because we've gotten into a habit of notating books and building our own business libraries for future reference. Discuss these ideas with your friends on Facebook, Twitter, and other social media platforms. Never forget—*your value to an organization is your ability to have the answers.* So do whatever it takes to become a valuable change resource for your company, your associates, and your friends.

3. *Never stop the journey of "change mastery" in your own life.* The concept of "mastery" is something the ancients held in very high regard. Becoming an expert, being the best, or achieving greatness is all part of this concept, but true mastery is mental, physical, *and* spiritual. Mastery is a journey, so don't think it's something to ever be fully achieved, but rather, it's a lifelong process of learning and growing. The great Russian novelist Leo Tolstoy said, "Everyone thinks of changing the world, but no one thinks of changing himself." Always be open to new ideas, new

information, and new ways of accomplishing your dreams. Shake things up. Jolt the thinking of those around you. Keep pointing out the elephants in the room. This is a spiritual journey that causes you to constantly evaluate yourself and your purpose in the world, and it should continue as long as you live and breathe.

A blockbuster movie is a movie that dominates the competition, influences the culture, generates incredible income, sets records, and jolts the industry. A *blockbuster life* is a life that does all that and more. From this moment on, view every person and every situation you encounter through the eyes of change. Commit your life to embracing disruption and chaos as they happen and igniting change where it is needed.

> *Either you decide to stay in the shallow end of the pool*
> *or you go out into the ocean.*
> —CHRISTOPHER REEVE, ACTOR AND ACTIVIST FOR THE HANDICAPPED

Change is about intervention. Rosa Parks sat in the back of a bus a hundred times in Montgomery, Alabama, before she made the decision to move up. That decision ignited a change that jolted a nation.

Change is something that happens one person at a time, in unexpected moments, and often has far greater impact than anyone could dream.

As Gandhi said, "You must be the change you wish to see in the world."

The world is changing. Now, so can you.

Be the change, make change happen, and never look back.

Jolt your life!

REVIEW
Jolt Your Future

1. In what areas of my life can I learn from failure? (Remember, a mistake is just another option.)
2. It's not about me. Who are the people who can perform on my team? Whom can I turn to for advice, creative ideas, and encouragement?
3. How can I personally be a better team member?
4. What kind of legacy will I leave?
5. What can I do now to leave a legacy to be proud of?
6. How can I increase the power and value of my personal influence?
7. How can I use my influence to change my networks, my community, and potentially the world?

ACKNOWLEDGMENTS

L ooking back to the the start of my career, this was not anywhere close to where I thought I would be at this point in my life. And yet I've had the remarkable opportunity to be married to a woman who was willing to stick with me for the duration. Kathleen is my wife, business partner, coach, and confidante and the mother of our children. Her influence on this book has been enormous, to the point of even letting me test some of my wacky theories out on her. To say "thank you" would never express the difference she's made in my life, but if we sell any books, I'll make it up with that vacation I've been promising.

Our children, Bailey and Kelsey, and Kelsey's husband, Chris, have lived with my travel schedule, and grown up with me bouncing around the world. In spite of that, they are living life to its fullest, and we couldn't be more proud. Had I known they'd turn out so well, we'd have had a few more.

None of this would have happened without the incredible clients I've had the opportunity to work with over the years. They allowed me the laboratory to explore these ideas, push for answers, and never settle for second best. There's no question that as we changed your organizations, you changed my life as well.

Finally, to my literary agents, Rachelle Gardner and Greg Johnson: thanks for believing not just in this idea but in me. Your advice, guidance, and a few timely "jolts" have kept this project on course. And to the team at Thomas Nelson publishers—Joel Miller, Bryan Norman, David Schroeder, and CEO Michael Hyatt—this has truly been a great publishing experience.

Phil Cooke

September 12, 2010

CREDITS

Block, Peter. *The Answer to How Is Yes: Acting on What Matters*. San Francisco: Berrett-Koehler, 2003.

Branden, Nathaniel. *The Psychology of Self-Esteem*. New York: Jossey-Bass, 2001.

Bronson, Po and Ashley Merryman. *NurtureShock*. New York: Hatchett Book Group, 2009.

Colbert, Don. *Deadly Emotions*. Nashville: Thomas Nelson, 2003.

Collins, Jim. *Good to Great*. New York: HarperCollins, 2001.

Croyden, Margaret. *Conversations with Peter Brook*. New York: Faber and Faber, 2003.

Downes, Larry, and Chunka Mui. *Unleashing the Killer App*. Boston: Harvard Business School Press, 1998.

Doyle, Patrick. Accessed at University of Waterloo, Conflict, Culture and Memory Lab. http://ccmlab.uwaterloo.ca/pad/corporate.html#domvid.

Flew, Antony. Quoted in Sturat Wavell and Will Iredale. "Sorry, says athiest-in-chief, I do believe in God after all. *The Sunday Times*, Dec. 12, 2004.

Fisher, David. *The War Magician*. New York: Berkley Books, 1983.

Freeman, John. *The Tyranny of E-Mail*. New York: Scribner, 2009.

Hamel, Gary. "Bringing Silicon Valley Inside." *Harvard Business Review*. September–October 1999.

Hawkins, Jeff. "Voices of Innovation." *Bloomberg Businessweek*. http://www.businessweek.com/magazine/content/04_41/b3903464.html.

Hymowitz, Kay. "What the Experts Are Saying." *Wall Street Journal*. August 25, 2009.

Ionesco, Eugène. *Present Past, Past Present*. New York: Grove Press, 1971.

Johnston, Robert K. *Useless Beauty: Ecclesiastes Through the Lens of Contemporary Film*. Grand Rapids: Baker Academic, 2004.

Kantrowitz, Barbara, and Karen Springen. "What Dreams Are Made Of." *Newsweek*, August 9, 2004.

Kelley, Tom. *The Art of Innovation*. New York: Doubleday, 2001.

Last, Jonathan V. "Killjoys for Change." *Weekly Standard*. June 14, 2010.

Phelps, Elizabeth. Quoted in Denise Prince Martin. "Being Afraid Is All in Your Mind." *Psychology Today*, September 1, 2001.

McCain, John. "In Search of Courage." *Fast Company*, September 1, 2004. http://www.fastcompany.com/magazine/86/mccain.html.

McClellan, Steve. "Ad Biz Faces the 'New Normal.' " *ADWEEK*, August 3, 2009. http://www.adweek.com/aw/content_display/news/agency/e3ia2224c3f78e5a3ce8f0edef5e540cd3d?pn=1.

Monahan, Tom. *The Do-It-Yourself Lobotomy*. New York: John Wiley & Sons, 2002.

Omartian, Stormie. *The Power of a Praying Woman*. Eugene, OR: Harvest House, 2002.

Qualman, Erik. *Socialnomics*. New York: John Wiley & Sons, 2009.

Robbins, Anthony. *Awaken the Giant Within*. New York: Free Press, 1991.

Sanders, Tim. *Love Is the Killer App*. New York: Three Rivers Press, 2002.

Sweet, Leonard. *SoulTsunami: Sink or Swim in New Millennium Culture*. Grand Rapids: Zondervan, 1999.

Van Allsburg, Chris. *The Polar Express*. New York: Houghton Mifflin, 1985.

Wavell, Stuart, and Will Iredale. "Sorry, says atheist-in-chief, I do believe in God after all." *London Sunday Times*, December 12, 2004.

ABOUT THE AUTHOR

Phil Cooke, a writer, speaker, and filmmaker, is changing the way business, church, and nonprofit leaders influence and engage the culture. *Christianity Today* calls him a "media guru." His media company, Cooke Pictures, advises many of the largest and most effective churches and nonprofit organizations in the world. A founding partner in the commercial production company TWC Films, he also produces national advertising for some of the largest companies in the country. His books and online blog at philcooke.com are changing the way religious and nonprofit organizations tell their stories. He's lectured at universities such as Yale, University of California at Berkeley, and UCLA and is an adjunct professor at the King's College and Seminary and Biola University in Los Angeles.

Find out more at philcooke.com.

THANKS FOR READING *JOLT!*

I hope it's inspired you to realize the incredible potential that a good jolt can give to your dreams and your future. In your journey toward accomplishing things, I would love to hear your story. Just visit www.joltyourlife.com and share your story about how it's going. Plus, get a book for a friend who could use a good jolt as well.

—Phil Cooke